BRIEF ENCOUNTER

BRIEF ENCOUNTER

Noël Coward

faber and faber
LONDON·NEW YORK

First published in 1974
by Lorrimer Publishing Limited.

Published in 1990 in the collection
Masterworks of the British Cinema
by Faber and Faber Limited
3 Queen Square London WC1N 3AU

Published in the United States by Faber and Faber, Inc.,
a division of Farrar, Straus and Giroux, Inc., New York

This Classic Screenplays edition published in 1999

Printed in England by Clays Ltd, St Ives plc

A CIP record for this book
is available from the British Library

ISBN 0–571–19680–2

2 4 6 8 10 9 7 5 3 1

CONTENTS

INTRODUCTION

The story of *Brief Encounter* does not begin with the making of film in 1945, though it was on 2 June of that year that Noël wrote in his diary 'Saw very rough cut of *Brief Encounter*, delighted with it. Celia (Johnson) quite wonderful, Trevor Howard fine and obviously a new star. Whole thing beautifully played and directed – and, let's face it, beautifully written.'

It had in fact been written, in a somewhat different form, fully ten years earlier. Back in 1935, Noël was looking for a stage vehicle for himself and Gertrude Lawrence, one with which they could repeat the success they had first enjoyed in 1930 when *Private Lives*, both in the West End and on Broadway, had turned them into 'Noël and Gertie', the most successful stage partnership of their era.

The need for the new vehicle was paramount and twofold; Gertie had to be rescued from her recent bankruptcy hearings, and Noël wished to consolidate their partnership, one which had started in 1911 on Euston station when both were child actors travelling north; now he was also trying to circumvent the very real boredom that each of them felt playing the same script eight times a week for several months. Better than one play would surely be three; better than three would be nine.

Thus was born the unique idea of *Tonight at 8.30*; a cycle of nine one-act plays to be performed at alternate evening and matinée performances in sets of three. Each set was to contain one short musical, one comedy and one drama, and in the end six of the plays were to end up on film, three as separate full-length features, and three in an omnibus collection called *Meet Me Tonight* (1952).

But only one of these was to make a real screen impact. Originally entitled *Still Life*, it was set in the railway station buffet at Milford Junction and told the story of a middle-aged, married doctor and the equally middle-aged, married housewife with whom he falls hopelessly in love. 'Of all the plays in *Tonight at 8.30*,' wrote Noel in his original preface to them, 'this was by far the most mature; later it was made into an excellent film and retitled *Brief Encounter*. I am fond of both the play and the film with, as usual, a slight bias in favour of the former. It is well-written, economical and well-constructed; the characters, I think, are true, and I can say now, reading it with detachment after so many years, that I am proud to have written it.'

Noël's 'slight bias' in favour of the play was, at the time of writing in 1954, certainly understandable; he had not yet moved into the last, golden period of his character-acting on screen (*Around The World in 80 Days*, *Our Man in Havana*, *Bunny Jake Is Missing*, *The Italian Job*, etc.), and although his relationship with the silver screen had started as early as 1917, when, at the age of sixteen, he had made his face up bright green and pushed a wheelbarrow down a street in Hertfordshire with Lillian and Dorothy Gish for D. W. Griffith's World War I epic *Hearts of the World*, it had not thus far been a very happy one.

Hitchcock had filmed *The Vortex* with Ivor Novello as an unsatisfactory silent in 1927, Robert Montgomery and Norma Shearer had made a mess of *Private Lives* in 1931, Nelson Eddy and Jeannette Macdonald had made a travesty of *Bitter Sweet* in 1941 and several other of his more or less beloved scripts had been in one way or another destroyed by film-makers on both sides of the Atlantic. By the time it came to *We Were Dancing* from *Tonight at 8.30*, all that Hollywood bothered to keep was the title.

Indeed the only film that had given Noël any real pleasure in the years before World War Two was the one that remains his least known, *The Scoundrel*, a curiously fascinating 1935 Ben Hecht drama shot in New York with Noël as a publisher returning from death by drowning and Julie Hayden as his lost love.

But in July 1941, Noël's relationship with the cinema was to change drastically. Until then, his war work had been by his own definition somewhat shaky; cancelling rehearsals for no less than three new plays (*Blithe Spirit*, *This Happy Breed* and *Present Laughter*) at the onset of hostilities in 1939, he had been sent to Paris on an obscure propaganda mission, thence to Washington, and eventually told by Churchill that the best and most useful thing he could do would be to carry on singing 'Mad Dogs & Englishmen' at troop concerts around the various fronts. Willing and able to do this, Noël still did not feel he was being inventively or properly used, and it wasn't until his lifelong friend Louis Mountbatten relayed the story of the sinking of HMS *Kelly* under his own command that Noël suddenly began to see the outline of something he could usefully contribute to the war effort.

Mountbatten was always as keen to propagate his own image as was Noël, whom he in many ways much resembled, and it soon occurred to the two men that from the jaws of the *Kelly* defeat could be dragged a kind of victory – a major feature film, originally entitled 'White Ensign', which would tell the story of Mountbatten and the *Kelly* and celebrate the Royal Navy at war in a way that had never yet been achieved.

The film, soon retitled *In Which We Serve*, ran into considerable bureaucratic opposition, not least from those who already resented Mountbatten's undeniably showbiz sense of personal survival, but eventually approval was given, largely through the intervention of Churchill himself, and production began in December 1941. Apart from his work as the screenwriter, Noël was to star as the Mountbatten character and also, for the very first time, to direct.

As Kevin Brownlow indicates in his brilliant and definitive *David Lean* biography, the genesis of *In Which We Serve* was one of those moments in the history of the British cinema when all kinds of disparate characters suddenly found common cause. Coward himself, having written and directed the stage epic *Cavalcade* a decade earlier, wanted to do something similarly patriotic for the Navy at war; Mountbatten wanted a face-saving propaganda picture from which he could emerge as hero; Filippo del Guidice, a flamboyant Italian producer only recently released from wartime internment, was looking for his 'big picture' (he was to go on to the Olivier *Henry V*), and Noël even had some official credentials for the project in that only a few months earlier he had been detailed by the Royal Naval Film Corporation to visit battleships checking up on the kinds of movies sailors wished to see aboard.

This, he felt, gave him all the background he needed to turn Mountbatten's true-life misadventure with the *Kelly* into a more generic picture about naval heroism, and the way that a ship could even replace a family in the hearts of men. The screenplay also allowed him to settle an old score with his arch enemy Lord Beaverbrook; as the newly commissioned HMS *Torrin* (screen version of the *Kelly*) sails down the Clyde on the way to battle stations, she passes an old *Daily Express* front page floating in the water. THERE WILL BE NO WAR is the headline, and Beaverbrook never forgave Coward for the way he immortalized an embarrassing mistake on screen for all time.

But almost as soon as he began to write, Noël became aware of his central problem; a jack of all entertainment trades who was already the Master of most, even he realized that to write, direct (for the very first time) and star in a major feature film, already controversial in subject matter, would be a tricky triple to realize. He needed considerable help, and he already knew where to find it; meticulous as ever in preparations, once he knew that his film had the go-ahead, he made it his business to watch several other films of the period to see precisely who was doing what on screen and how successfully. From this immersion in the British cinema of the early 1940s, he emerged with three key names: those of the producer Anthony Havelock-

Allan, the cinematographer Ronald Neame, and the editor David Lean. All three men were, Noël decided, to be his key aides and tutors, and they in turn gave him a crash course in the rudiments of writing (and acting) for screen rather than stage.

It was soon agreed that Lean would work as Noël's co-director, a role of crucial importance given how much of the time Coward himself was to be in front of the camera, and shooting started immediately after Christmas 1941, with the news of Pearl Harbor and the imminent fall of Singapore giving any war picture constant topicality and energy. 'Day spent doing scenes over and over again,' reads an entry in Noël's diary for 6 January 1942, 'trying to eliminate Noël Coward mannerisms. Saw yesterday's rushes and was for the first time pleased with my performance and my appearance. Ronnie (Neame) has at last discovered what to do about my face, which is to photograph it from above rather than below.'

Already it was clear that Noël, although the film's star, originator, writer and spokesman in all the debates that were continuing with a grudging War Office about the film's 'suitability' as propaganda (a sinking ship is after all not the greatest of images for triumph at sea), was essentially going to do the acting while Lean and Neame did the shooting and the post-production. This Noël was the first to acknowledge, writing in his diary a few month's later, when the film was awarded a special Oscar, 'I am so pleased for dear Ronnie and David, who richly deserve this.'

From Lean's point of view, *In When We Serve* was the film which won him his director's ticket, and for that he was more than willing to take a co-directing credit with Noël, especially as it duly led to the founding of Cineguild, a partnership of Neame, Lean and Havelock-Allan specifically founded in 1942 with Noël's blessing for the filming of such of his plays as were deemed suitable for the screen, or as yet untouched by it.

Thus it was that Cineguild filmed two of Noël's most successful recent stage scripts, *This Happy Breed* (with Robert Newton and Celia Johnson) and *Blithe Spirit* (with Rex Harrison and, from the stage cast, Kay Hammond and Margaret Rutherford) in quick succession in 1942–3. Then, thinking it was perhaps time to break at least temporarily with Noël, the Cineguild trio began to work on a Mary Queen of Scots project, at least until Noël told them that none of them knew anything about costume history and he would have another modern–dress script ready for them in a matter of days.

This, it turned out, was his extended version of *Still Life*, already retitled *Brief Encounter* and now rewritten with considerable input from Lean and Neame, indeed so much that their producer Havelock-Allan was later to imply all the new material came from the three of them, rather than Noël himself. This dispute has never been satisfactorily resolved, though I would suggest that if you now were to take the trouble to read the screenplay which follows in conjunction with the (also newly republished) text of *Still Life*, you would find in the 'extra' scenes passages of dialogue so quintessentially Cowardesque that if Havelock-Allan is right, he and his two partners were amazingly accurate and stylish ghost-writers.

This is not to suggest that Havelock-Allan is altogether wrong; there are clearly some scenes in *Brief Encounter* which are not Noël's original writing, and others in which the Cineguild trio evidently dictated to Coward the needs of a particular sequence for the camera and then had him write to order.

As to the casting, with Gertrude Lawrence now living and working in America with her second husband, Richard Aldrich, and Noël himself still heavily committed to troop concerts, there was no question of reassembling the original stage cast of *Still Life*, nor might the Cineguild trio, who were still patiently trying to teach Coward that the cinema was something rather more than a way of photographing stage plays, have wanted to. Instead they turned to their beloved Celia Johnson (from both *In Which We Serve* and *This Happy Breed*) and then first to Roger Livesey for the married doctor.

When Livesey proved unavailable, their second choice was a young actor just starting to make his screen name, primarily for playing the young Squadron Leader who gets killed at the start of *The Way to the Stars*. He was Trevor Howard, a stage actor of considerable style who had been invalided out of the army in 1943 for what were called 'psychiatric' reasons, one parachute-regiment doctor going so far as to describe him as 'psychopathic'. This did not, unsurprisingly, thrill Howard or his highly respectable parents, so when another Trevor Howard subsequently won the MC, they allowed the press to assume it was the actor, who never strove officiously to deny the award, which was referred to in many of his glowing reviews for *Brief Encounter*.

Other Coward 'regulars', including Noël's beloved friend Joyce Carey and (from *This Happy Breed*) Stanley Holloway, were recruited for supporting roles, but Celia took a dim view of the film's prospects in a letter to her husband Peter Fleming:

> It's about a woman, married with two children, who meets by chance a man in a railway waiting-room and they fall in love. And it's All No Good. It will be pretty unadulterated Johnson, and when I am not being sad or anguished or renouncing, I am narrating about it. So if they don't have

my beautiful face to look at, they will always have my mellifluous voice to listen to. Lucky people.

Celia's nerves were not helped by the sudden realization that (though she would still take second billing to the relative newcomer Howard), for the first time it was she, as the established star, who would effectively be carrying the picture:

I am scared stiff of the film, and get first-night 'indijaggers' before every shot, but perhaps I'll get over that. It's going to be most awfully difficult – you need to be a star of the silent screen, because there's such a lot of stuff with commentary over it and that's terribly difficult to do.

The original intention had been to shoot *Brief Encounter* at a London railway station, but it was then decided the crew would be too likely to get in the way of troop transports and other priorities, so they went instead to Carnforth in Lancashire, less busy and less prone to air raids, besides having a highly suitable and as yet undamaged railway station.

There were the usual early crises; Noël's first choice for the chattering friend who interrupts the lovers' farewell meeting had been the actress Joyce Barbour, whose camera fright was such that she had to be replaced late in the shooting by Everley Gregg. Then Coward decided that his regular and beloved designer Gladys Calthrop's costumes were far too grand for an essentially downmarket and even suburban story, so they had to be changed, but after that all went reasonably well, even when they returned for the interiors to Celia's 'dear old Denham'.

Howard found it hard to understand why his character fails to take Johnson to bed when he first has the chance, and had to be given a masterclass in sexual restraint by Lean; later, several critics, and David himself, admitted they were embarrassed by the cockney 'comic relief' scenes with Joyce Carey as the tea lady and Stanley Holloway as the station master, but Coward the craftsman knew enough to realize that comic relief, from Shakespeare's time onwards, had always been an essential feature of drama.

Although Howard was later to note that he would 'hate only to be remembered for *Brief Encounter*,' there is no doubt that this was the defining moment of his career, and for Celia too it was the film by which she would always be remembered, though she also had doubts about how it would be received; better perhaps in France, where films like Charles Boyer and Michele Morgan's *L'Orage* (1938) had already pioneered the quiet, doomed romance:

'Ours is of course much more English,' wrote Celia, 'and I can't decide if it's good or not. Some bits come off very well, but what I can't be sure is if the story is strong enough. I'm not bad in some bits, rotten in others ... all the music will help, especially with Rachmaninoff's Piano Concerto swishing through it ... perhaps people can hum it to themselves. That might help.'

In the event, *Brief Encounter* was something of a 'sleeper'; when the first print was ready, Lean was already shooting his next film, *Great Expectations*, on the Romney Marshes and unwisely decided to organize a sneak preview at Rochester, where to his horror the love scenes were greeted with uproarious laughter:

'I remember', said Lean, 'going back to my hotel room and lying in bed almost in tears thinking "How can I get into the laboratory at Denham and burn the negative?", I was that ashamed of it.'

But from Rochester, things could only get better; London critics were almost unanimous in praise, and their doyenne C. A. Lejeune even chose it on radio as her 'Desert Island' film, the only one she could not bear to live without: 'It seems to me', she wrote, 'to catch in words and pictures so many things that are penetratingly true. The whole colour, the spring, the almost magical feeling of the discovery that someone's in love with you; that someone feels it's exciting to be with you; that is something so tenuous that it is hardly ever put on the screen.'

Brief Encounter has had a curious afterlife; in 1947 BBC radio presented it with the original cast; in 1954 Trevor Howard starred in an American radio version opposite Ginger Rogers, not perhaps the likeliest of casting; and in 1974 there was a truly terrible wide-screen remake with Richard Burton and Sophia Loren, while in 1980, close to the end of their careers, Trevor and Celia were reunited for the television version of Paul Scott's *Staying On*, which could well have been considered the story of their original *Brief Encounter* couple had they not parted, at least in the view of the film historian Kevin Brownlow, who also recalls an all-gay film version called *Flames of Passion*.

As for David, he remained for many months in doubt about the film's eventual reception:

We defied all the rules of box-office success; there were no big star names. There was an unhappy ending to the main love story. The film was played in unglamorous surroundings. And the two leading characters were approaching middle age. A few years ago this would have been a recipe for box-office disaster, but this wasn't the case with *Brief Encounter*. The film did very well in this country in what are known as 'the better-class halls' and it had a similar success, but on a smaller scale, in New York.

It ran there for eight months, and Lean was the first director of a British film since Korda before the war to get an Oscar nomination; he and Neame and Havelock-Allan also got nominated for their screenplay; Celia Johnson got a nomination, though none that year brought home the actual statue.

And that, give or take a memorable Mike Nichols/Elaine May cabaret parody, was more or less that; more than half a century after it was made, *Brief Encounter* stands as the first truly modern, European/British movie in which words count for more than action, and psychology replaces physical jerks. It also however marked the break-up of the partnership of Noël Coward and David Lean; Lean now wished to be 'set free' to pursue other interests in the filming of Charles Dickens. Noël set him free with his customary, elegant good grace, never once remarking that had it not been for him, Lean would never have made the breakthrough from editor to director.

Three brief reviews to end:

'*Brief Encounter* is a pleasure to watch as a well controlled piece of work, at the same time deeply touching.' James Agee

'Polished as this film is, its strength does not lie in movie technique (of which there is plenty), so much as in the tight realism of its detail.' Richard Winnington

'A celebrated, craftsmanlike tearjerker, and incredibly neat. There is not a breath of air in it.' Pauline Kael

Sheridan Morley,
September 98

Sheridan Morley is the drama critic of the *Spectator* and the *International Herald Tribune*. He also presents Radio 2's *Arts Programme*, reviews regularly for London Weekend Televisions's *Theatreland*, and has presented many arts programmes for BBC television and radio. He won the Arts Journalist of the Year in 1990, and was nominated for a Grammy in same year. He is the author of numerous biographies and studies, including the first biography of Noël Coward, *A Talent to Amuse* (1969).

In researching this new Preface, Sheridan Morley would like to acknowledge Kevin Brownlow's monumental and definitive *David Lean* (Faber and

Faber, 1997); *The Noël Coward Diaries* (Weidenfeld 1999, edited by Graham Payn and Sheridan Morley); *Celia Johnson* by Kate Fleming (Weidenfeld, 1991); and *Trevor Howard* by Michael Munn (Robson, 1989).

BRIEF ENCOUNTER

BRIEF ENCOUNTER

The action of this film takes place during the winter of 1938-39. It is early evening. A local train is pulling into platform Number 1 of Milford Junction Station, as a voice over the loudspeaker announces:

LOUDSPEAKER: *Milford Junction — Milford Junction.*

The train comes closer and closer, and a great cloud of steam is hissed out from the engine. The screen becomes completely white as the main titles appear. With the last title the steam disperses, revealing again the engine, which starts to pull out of the station. ALBERT GODBY is at the ticket barrier. He is somewhere between 30 and 40 years old. His accent is north country. He collects the last few tickets from the passengers of the departing train and moves towards the edge of the platform. An express train is approaching from the distance. ALBERT jumps down from platform Number 1 onto the track, and waits for the express to pass. It roars by, practically blotting out the view. ALBERT watches the train pass, as the lights from the carriage windows flash across his face. From his waistcoat pocket he takes out a watch and chain, and checks the time of the train. The watch reads 5.35. By the look of satisfaction on his face we know that the train is punctual. He puts the watch back and the lights cease flashing on his face. The train has passed, and ALBERT follows it with his eyes as it roars into the tunnel. He crosses the line over which the express has just gone by, jumps onto platform Number 2, and moves towards the refreshment room.

Inside the refreshment room he crosses to the counter, behind which stand MYRTLE BAGOT and her assistant BERYL WATERS. MYRTLE is a buxom and imposing widow. Her hair is piled high, and her expression is reasonably jaunty except on those occasions when a strong sense of refinement gets the better of her. BERYL is pretty but dimmed, not only by MYRTLE's personal effulgence, but by her firm authority.

ALBERT: *Hullo! — Hullo! — Hullo!*

MYRTLE: *Quite a stranger, aren't you?*
ALBERT: *I couldn't get in yesterday.*
MYRTLE bridling: *I wondered what happened to you.*
ALBERT: *I 'ad a bit of a dust-up.*
MYRTLE preparing his tea: *What about?*
ALBERT: *Saw a chap getting out of a first-class compartment, and when he comes to give up 'is ticket it was third-class, and I told 'im he'd have to pay excess, and then he turned a bit nasty and I 'ad to send for Mr Saunders.*
MYRTLE: *Fat lot of good he'd be.*
ALBERT: *He ticked him off proper.*
MYRTLE: *Seein's believing. . . .*

In the far end of the refreshment room, seated at a table, are ALEC HARVEY and LAURA JESSON. He is about 35 and wears a mackintosh and squash hat. She is an attractive woman in her thirties. Her clothes are not smart, but obviously chosen with taste. They are in earnest conversation, but we do not hear what they are saying.

ALBERT off: *I tell you, he ticked 'im off proper — ' You pay the balance at once,' he said, ' or I'll 'and you over to the police.' You should 'ave seen the chap's face at the mention of the word ' police '. Changed his tune then 'e did — paid up quick as lightning.*
MYRTLE off: *That's just what I mean. He hadn't got the courage to handle it himself. He had to call in the police.*
ALBERT off: *Who said he called in the police?*
MYRTLE off: *You did, of course.*
ALBERT off: *I didn't do any such thing. I merely said he mentioned the police, which is quite a different thing from calling them in. He's not a bad lot, Mr Saunders. After all, you can't expect much spirit from a man who's only got one lung and a wife with diabetes.*
MYRTLE off: *I thought something must be wrong when you didn't come.*

Close shot of ALBERT and MYRTLE. BERYL is in the background. Close shots of ALBERT and MYRTLE individually, as they are speaking.

ALBERT: *I'd have popped in to explain, but I had a date, and 'ad to run for it the moment I went off.*
MYRTLE frigidly: *Oh, indeed!*
ALBERT: *A chap I know's getting married.*

MYRTLE: *Very interesting, I'm sure.*

ALBERT: *What's up with you, anyway?*

MYRTLE: *I'm sure I don't know to what you're referring.*

ALBERT: *You're a bit unfriendly all of a sudden.*

MYRTLE ignoring him: *Beryl, hurry up — put some coal in the stove while you're at it.*

BERYL: *Yes, Mrs Bagot.*

MYRTLE: *I'm afraid I really can't stand here wasting my time in idle gossip, Mr Godby.*

ALBERT: *Aren't you going to offer me another cup?*

MYRTLE: *You can 'ave another cup and welcome when you've finished that one. Beryl 'll give it to you — I've got my accounts to do.*

ALBERT: *I'd rather you gave it to me.*

MYRTLE: *Time and tide wait for no man, Mr Godby.*

ALBERT: *I don't know what you're huffy about, but whatever it is I'm very sorry.*

> DOLLY is seen at the counter. Forgetting her tea, she hurries across the room to join LAURA and ALEC.

DOLLY: *Laura! What a lovely surprise!*

LAURA dazed: *Oh, Dolly!*

DOLLY: *My dear, I've shopped until I'm dropping! My feet are nearly falling off, and my throat's parched. I thought of having tea in Spindle's but I was terrified of losing the train. I'm always missing trains, and being late for meals, and Bob gets disagreeable for days at a time — he's been getting those dreadful headaches you know — I've been trying to make him see a doctor, but he won't. Flopping down at their table: Oh, dear.*

LAURA: *This is Doctor Harvey.*

ALEC rising: *How do you do!*

DOLLY shaking hands: *How do you do. Would you be a perfect dear and get me my cup of tea? I don't think I could drag my poor old bones back to the counter again. I must get some chocolates for Tony, too, but I can do that afterwards.*

> She offers him money.

ALEC waving it away: *No, please. . . .*

> He goes drearily out of frame towards the counter.
> Close shot of DOLLY and LAURA.

DOLLY: *My dear — what a nice-looking man. Who on earth is he?*

5

Really, you're quite a dark horse. I shall telephone Fred in the morning and make mischief — this is a bit of luck. I haven't seen you for ages, and I've been meaning to pop in, but Tony's had measles, you know, and I had all that awful fuss about Phyllis —

LAURA with an effort: *Oh, how dreadful!*

At the counter, ALEC is standing next to ALBERT, who is finishing his cup of tea. ALBERT leaves and MYRTLE hands ALEC the change for DOLLY's cup of tea.

DOLLY off: *Mind you, I never cared for her much, but still Tony did. Tony adored her, and — but never mind, I'll tell you all about that in the train.*

ALEC picks up DOLLY's tea and moves back to the table. He sits down again.

DOLLY: *Thank you so very much. They've certainly put enough milk in it — but still, it'll be refreshing.* She sips it. *Oh, dear — no sugar.*

ALEC: *It's in the spoon.*

DOLLY: *Oh, of course — what a fool I am — Laura, you look frightfully well. I do wish I'd known you were coming in today, we could have come together and lunched and had a good gossip. I loathe shopping by myself anyway.*

There is the sound of a bell on the platform, and a loudspeaker voice announces the arrival of the Churley train.

LAURA: *There's your train.*

ALEC: *Yes, I know.*

DOLLY: *Aren't you coming with us?*

ALEC: *No, I go in the opposite direction. My practice is in Churley.*

DOLLY: *Oh, I see.*

ALEC: *I'm a general practitioner at the moment.*

LAURA dully: *Doctor Harvey is going out to Africa next week.*

DOLLY: *Oh, how thrilling.*

There is the sound of ALEC's train approaching.

ALEC: *I must go.*

LAURA: *Yes, you must.*

ALEC: *Good-bye.*

DOLLY: *Good-bye.*

ALEC shakes hands with DOLLY, looks at LAURA swiftly once, and gives her shoulder a little squeeze. The train is heard rumbling into the station. He goes over to the door and out onto the platform.

LAURA is gazing at the door through which ALEC has just passed. She seems unaware of the chattering DOLLY at her side, who proceeds to fumble in her handbag for lipstick and a mirror. Close shot of LAURA.

DOLLY: *He'll have to run or he'll miss it — he's got to get right over to the other platform. Talking of missing trains reminds me of that awful bridge at Broadham Junction — you have to go traipsing all up one side, along the top and down the other! Well, last week I'd been over to see Bob's solicitor about renewing the lease of the house — and I arrived at the station with exactly half a minute to spare. . . .*

Close shot of DOLLY, who is applying lipstick to her chattering mouth and watching the operation in her little hand-mirror.

DOLLY: *. . . My dear, I flew — I had Tony with me, and like a fool, I'd brought a new shade for the lamp in the drawing-room — I could just as easily have got it here in Milford.*

Close shot of LAURA.

DOLLY off: *. . . It was the most enormous thing and I could hardly see over it — I've never been in such a frizz in my life — I nearly knocked a woman down.*

The door onto the platform is seen from LAURA'S point of view.

DOLLY off: *. . . Of course, by the time I got it home it was battered to bits.*

There is the sound of a bell on the platform as we resume on LAURA and DOLLY.

DOLLY: *Is that a train?*

She addresses MYRTLE.

DOLLY: *Can you tell me, is that the Ketchworth train?*

MYRTLE off: *No, that's the express.*

LAURA: *The boat-train.*

DOLLY: *Oh, yes — that doesn't stop, does it?*

She gets up and crosses to MYRTLE at the counter.

DOLLY: *Express trains are Tony's passion in life — I want some chocolate, please.*

MYRTLE: *Milk or plain?*

DOLLY: *Plain, I think — or no, perhaps milk would be nicer. Have you any with nuts in it?*

The express is heard in the distance.

MYRTLE: *Nestle's nut-milk — shilling or sixpence?*

DOLLY: *Give me one plain and one nut-milk.*

The noise of the express sounds louder. The express roa[...] through the station as DOLLY finishes buying and paying f[...] her chocolate. She turns to see that LAURA is no longer at t[...] table.

DOLLY: *Oh, where is she?*

MYRTLE looking over the counter: *I never noticed her go.*

There is the sound of a door opening and they both look u[...] LAURA comes in through the door from Number 2 platforr[...] looking very white and shaky. She shuts the door and lea[...] back against it. DOLLY enters frame.

DOLLY: *My dear, I couldn't think where you'd disappeared to.*

LAURA: *I just wanted to see the express go through.*

DOLLY: *What on earth's the matter? Do you feel ill?*

LAURA: *I feel a little sick.*

LAURA goes slowly over to the table, where DOLLY helps he[...] into a chair. The platform bell goes and the loudspeaker a[...] nounces the arrival of the Ketchworth train.

LAURA: *That's our train.*

DOLLY goes out of shot towards the counter.

DOLLY off: *Have you any brandy?*

MYRTLE off: *I'm afraid it's out of hours.*

DOLLY off: *Surely — if someone's feeling ill. . . .*

LAURA: *I'm all right really.*

Close shot of DOLLY and MYRTLE.

DOLLY: *Just a sip of brandy will buck you up.* To MYRTLE *Please. . . .*

MYRTLE: *Very well. . . .*

She pours out some brandy as the train is heard approachin[...] the station.

DOLLY: *How much?*

MYRTLE: *Tenpence, please.*

Resume on LAURA at the table.

DOLLY off: *There!*

The train is heard rumbling into the station. DOLLY moves int[...] frame with the brandy.

DOLLY: *Here you are, dear. (Still)*

LAURA taking it: *Thank you.*

She gulps down the brandy as DOLLY proceeds to gather up he[...]

8

parcels. They hurry across the refreshment room and out of the door leading to Number 3 platform.

Outside they cross the platform to the train. A porter opens the door of a third-class compartment. There is the sound of the door slamming, off. Through the carriage window at the far end can be seen platform Number 4. LAURA sits down and DOLLY bustles over to the corner seat opposite her.

DOLLY: *Well, this is a bit of luck, I must say....*

The carriage gives a jolt and the train starts to pull out of the station.

DOLLY: *... This train is generally packed.*

DOLLY, having placed her various packages on the seat beside her, leans forward to talk to LAURA.

DOLLY: *I really am worried about you, dear — you look terribly peaky.*

Close shot of LAURA over DOLLY's shoulder.

LAURA: *I'm all right — really I am — I just felt faint for a minute, that's all. It often happens to me you know — I once did it in the middle of Bobbie's school concert! I don't think he's ever forgiven me.*

She gives a little smile. It is obviously an effort, but she succeeds reasonably well.

Close shot of DOLLY over LAURA's shoulder.

DOLLY after a slight pause: *He was certainly very nice-looking.*

LAURA: *Who?*

DOLLY: *Your friend — that Doctor whatever his name was.*

Resume on LAURA, over DOLLY's shoulder.

LAURA: *Yes. He's a nice creature.*

DOLLY: *Have you known him long?*

LAURA: *No, not very long.*

LAURA smiles again, quite casually, but her eyes remain miserable.

LAURA: *I hardly know him at all, really....*

DOLLY off: *Well, my dear, I've always had a passion for doctors. I can well understand how it is that women get neurotic. Of course some of them go too far. I'll never forget that time Mary Norton had jaundice. The way she behaved with that doctor of hers was absolutely scandalous. Her husband was furious and said he would....*

9

DOLLY's words fade away. LAURA's mouth remains closed, bu
we hear her thoughts.

LAURA's VOICE: *I wish I could trust you. I wish you were a wise*
kind friend, instead of just a gossiping acquaintance that I've know
for years casually and never particularly cared for. . . . I wish. . . .
wish. . . .

Close shot of DOLLY over LAURA's shoulder.

DOLLY: *Fancy him going all the way to South Africa. Is he married*

LAURA: *Yes.*

DOLLY: *Any children?*

Close shot of LAURA.

LAURA: *Yes — two boys. He's very proud of them.*

DOLLY off: *Is he taking them with him, his wife and children?*

LAURA: *Yes — yes, he is.*

Close shot of DOLLY.

DOLLY: *I suppose it's sensible in a way — rushing off to start li*
anew in the wide open spaces, and all that sort of thing, but I mu
say wild horses wouldn't drag me away from England. . . .

Resume on LAURA.

DOLLY off: *. . . and home and all the things I'm used to — I mea*
one has one's roots after all, hasn't one?

LAURA: *Yes, one has one's roots.*

Close shot of DOLLY's mouth.

DOLLY: *A girl I knew years ago went out to Africa you know —*
her husband had something to do with engineering or somethin
and my dear. . . .

Close shot of LAURA.

DOLLY off: *She really had the most dreadful time — she got som*
awful kind of germ through going out on a picnic and she was
for months and months. . . .

DOLLY's voice has gradually faded away, and we hear LAURA
thoughts — her lips do not move.

LAURA's VOICE: *I wish you'd stop talking — I wish you'd stop pr*
ing and trying to find out things — I wish you were dead! No —
don't mean that — that was unkind and silly — but I wish you
stop talking. . . .

DOLLY's voice fades in again.

DOLLY off: *. . . all her hair came out and she said the social li*

was quite, quite horrid — provincial, you know, and very nouveau
riche. . . .

LAURA wearily: Oh, Dolly. . . .

Close shot of DOLLY over LAURA's shoulder.

DOLLY: What's the matter, dear — are you feeling ill again?

LAURA: No, not really ill, but a bit dizzy — I think I'll close my
eyes for a little.

DOLLY: Poor darling — what a shame and here am I talking away
nineteen to the dozen. I won't say another word and if you drop off
I'll wake you just as we get to the level crossing. That'll give you
time to pull yourself together and powder your nose before we get
out.

Close shot of LAURA.

LAURA: Thanks, Dolly.

She leans her head back and closes her eyes. The background
of the railway compartment darkens and becomes a misty
movement. The noise of the train fades away and music takes
its place.

LAURA's VOICE: This can't last — this misery can't last — I must
remember that and try to control myself. Nothing lasts really —
neither happiness nor despair — not even life lasts very long — there
will come a time in the future when I shan't mind about this any
more — when I can look back and say quite peacefully and cheerfully ' How silly I was ' — No, no, — I don't want that time to
come ever — I want to remember every minute — always — always
— to the end of my days. . . .

LAURA's head gives a sudden jerk as the train comes to a standstill.

DOLLY off: Wake up, Laura! We're here!

Simultaneously the background of the compartment comes back
to normal. Station lights flash past onto LAURA's face.

The music stops, and the screech of brakes takes its place.

A porter's voice is heard calling:

PORTER off: Ketchworth — Ketchworth — Ketchworth!

Dissolve to Ketchworth Station. It is night. LAURA and DOLLY
walk along the platform. The lights from the stationary train
illuminate their faces.

DOLLY: I could come to the house with you quite easily, you know
— it really isn't very much out of my way — all I have to do is to

cut through Elmore Lane — past the Grammar School and I shall b
home in two minutes.

LAURA: *It's sweet of you, Dolly, but I really feel perfectly all righ
now. That little nap in the train did wonders.*

DOLLY: *You're quite sure?*

LAURA: *Absolutely positive.*

    LAURA and DOLLY pass the barrier,. where they give up thei
tickets. A whistle blows and the train can be heard leaving th
station. They stop in the station yard beyond.

LAURA: *Thank you for being so kind.*

DOLLY: *Nonsense, dear. Well — I shall telephone in the mornin
to see if you've had a relapse.*

LAURA: *I shall disappoint you.* She kisses DOLLY. *Good night.*

DOLLY: *Good night — give my love to Fred and the children.*

    Dissolve to the exterior of LAURA's house. LAURA is see
approaching the gate of a solid. comfortable-looking hous
As she enters the gate, she feels in her handbag for her latch
key, finds it, opens the front door and goes inside.

    Seen from the hallway, LAURA enters the front door, glance
around, shuts the door quietly and moves out of shot toward
the stairs.

    The foreground of the shot is framed by a man's hat and coa
on a hat-stand. Beyond is the stairway and an open door lea
ing to the sitting-room. LAURA enters frame and starts to g
up the stairs.

FRED off, from the sitting-room: *Is that you, Laura?*

LAURA stopping on the stairs: *Yes, dear.*

FRED off: *Thank goodness you're back, the house has been in a
uproar.*

LAURA: *Why — what's the matter?*

FRED off: *Bobbie and Margaret have been fighting again, and the
won't go to sleep until you go in and talk to them about it.*

MARGARET off: *Mummy — Mummy! Is that you, Mummy?*

LAURA: *Yes, dear.*

BOBBIE off, from upstairs: *Come upstairs at once, Mummy — I wa
to talk to you.*

LAURA on the way upstairs again: *All right. I'm coming — but you'
both very naughty. You should be fast asleep by now.*

On the upstairs landing, LAURA crosses to the half-open door of the children's night nursery.

Inside the night nursery, the foreground is framed by two small twin beds. The room is in darkness and LAURA is silhouetted in the doorway.

LAURA: *Now what is it, you two?*

BOBBIE: *Well, Mummy, tomorrow's my birthday and I want to go to the circus, and tomorrow's not Margaret's birthday, and she wants to go to the pantomime, and I don't think it's fair.*

MARGARET: *I don't see why we've got to do everything Bobbie wants, just because it's his silly old birthday. Besides, my birthday is in June, and there aren't any pantomimes in June.*

BOBBIE persuasively: *Mummy, why don't you come and sit down on my bed?*

MARGARET: *No, Bobbie, Mummy's going to sit on my bed. She sat with you last night.*

LAURA: *I'm not going to sit with either of you. In fact I'm not going to come into the room. It's far too late to discuss it tonight, and if you don't go to sleep at once I shall tell Daddy not to let you go to either.*

BOBBIE and MARGARET together: *Oh, Mummy!*

Dissolve to the interior of the dining room. Close shot of LAURA and her husband FRED, who is a pleasant-looking man in his forties. They are seated at a round dining-room table and are just finishing their meal. LAURA is officiating at the Cona machine. (*Still*) The dining room is furnished comfortably without being in anyway spectacular.

FRED: *Why not take them to both? One in the afternoon and one in the evening?*

LAURA: *You know that's impossible. We shouldn't get home to bed until all hours — and they'd be tired and fractious.*

FRED: *One on one day, then, and the other on the other.*

LAURA handing him a cup of coffee: *Here you are, dear. You're always accusing me of spoiling the children. Their characters would be ruined in a month if I left them to your over-tender mercies.*

FRED cheerfully: *All right — have it your own way.*

Close shot of LAURA.

LAURA: *Circus or pantomime?*

FRED off: *Neither. We'll thrash them both soundly and lock them in the attic, and go to the cinema ourselves.*

LAURA's eyes suddenly fill with tears.

LAURA: *Oh, Fred!*

Close shot of FRED.

FRED: *What on earth's the matter?*

LAURA frantically dabbing her eyes: *Nothing — really it's nothing.*

FRED rises and crosses over to her. He puts his arms round her.

Close shot of FRED and LAURA.

FRED: *Darling — what's wrong? Please tell me. . . .*

LAURA: *Really and truly it's nothing — I'm just a little run-down. I had a sort of fainting spell in the refreshment room at Milford — wasn't it idiotic? Dolly Messiter was with me and talked and talked and talked until I wanted to strangle her — but still she meant to be kind — isn't it awful about people meaning to be kind? . . .*

FRED gently: *Would you like to go up to bed?*

LAURA: *No, Fred — really. . . .*

FRED: *Come and sit by the fire in the library and relax — you can help me with The Times crossword.*

LAURA forcing a smile: *You have the most peculiar ideas of relaxation.*

FRED: *That's better.*

LAURA rises with his arms still round her.

Dissolve to the interior of the library. FRED and LAURA are sitting on either side of the fire. FRED is in the foreground; on his lap is The Times, opened at the crossword puzzle. (*Still*) He holds a pencil in his hand. LAURA has some sewing to do. The library is cosy and intimate.

Close shots of LAURA and FRED individually, as they speak.

FRED: *But why a fainting spell? I can't understand it.*

LAURA: *Don't be so silly, darling — I've often had fainting spells and you know it. Don't you remember Bobbie's school concert and Eileen's wedding, and that time you insisted on taking me to that Symphony Concert in the Town Hall?*

FRED: *That was a nose bleed.*

LAURA: *I suppose I must just be that type of woman. It's very humiliating.*

FRED: *I still maintain that there'd be no harm in you seeing Doctor Graves.*

LAURA a little tremulously: *It would be a waste of time.*

FRED looks at her.

LAURA: *Do shut up about it, dear — you're making a fuss about nothing. I'd been shopping and I was tired and the refreshment room was very hot and I suddenly felt sick. Nothing more than that — really nothing more than that. Now get on with your old puzzle and leave me in peace.*

FRED: *All right — have it your own way.* After a pause: *You're a poetry addict — help me over this — it's Keats — ' When I behold upon the night starred face, huge cloudy symbols of a high' — something — in seven letters.*

LAURA with an effort: *Romance, I think — yes, I'm almost sure it is. ' Huge cloudy symbols of a high romance ' — It'll be in the Oxford Book of English Verse.*

FRED: *No that's right, I'm certain — it fits in with ' delirium ' and ' Baluchistan '.*

LAURA: *Will some music throw you off your stride?*

FRED: *No, dear — I'd like it.*

> LAURA crosses the room, turns on the radio and returns to her chair. She has tuned in to the opening movement of the Rachmaninoff Concerto in C minor.
>
> Close shot of LAURA. She takes up her sewing, then puts it down again and looks at her husband.
>
> Close shot of FRED. He is concentrating hard and scratching his head thoughtfully with the pencil.
>
> Close shot of LAURA, as her eyes fill with tears again. Her mouth remains closed but we hear her thoughts. . . .

LAURA'S VOICE: *Fred — Fred — dear Fred. There's so much that I want to say to you. You are the only one in the world with enough wisdom and gentleness to understand — if only it were somebody else's story and not mine. As it is you are the only one in the world that I can never tell — never — never — because even if I waited until we were old, old people, and told you then, you would be bound to look back over the years . . . and be hurt and oh, my dear, I don't want you to be hurt. You see, we are a happily married couple, and must never forget that. This is my home. . . .*

> A shot of FRED over LAURA's shoulder. He is engrossed in his crossword puzzle.

LAURA'S VOICE: *. . . you are my husband — and my children are upstairs in bed. I am a happily married woman — or rather, I was,*

*until a few weeks ago. This is my whole world and it is enough —
or rather, it was, until a few weeks ago.*

Close shot of LAURA.

LAURA'S VOICE: *. . . But, oh, Fred, I've been so foolish. I've fallen
in love! I'm an ordinary woman — I didn't think such violent things
could happen to ordinary people.*

Again a shot of FRED over LAURA's shoulder.

LAURA'S VOICE: *It all started on an ordinary day, in the most ordinary place in the world.*

The scene, with the exception of LAURA, slowly starts to dim
out. LAURA remains a solid figure in the foreground. As the room
fades away, the station refreshment room takes its place. LAURA,
as well as being in the foreground of the picture, is also seated
on one of the tables in the refreshment room, thus giving the
impression that she is watching herself. Dissolve.

It is now night time, about 5.30 p.m. The scene takes place in
the refreshment room at the Milford Junction Station. There
are only two or three other people in the room. MYRTLE and
BERYL are behind the counter, against which ALBERT is lolling,
sipping a cup of tea.

LAURA'S VOICE: *. . . the refreshment room at Milford Junction. I
was having a cup of tea and reading a book that I'd got that morning from Boots — my train wasn't due for ten minutes. . . . I looked
up and saw a man come in from the platform. He had on an ordinary
mac with a belt. His hat was turned down, and I didn't even see his
face. He got his tea at the counter and turned — then I did see his
face. It was rather a nice face. He passed my table on the way to his.
The woman at the counter was going on as usual. You know, I told
you about her the other day — the one with the refined voice. . . .*

Cut to MYRTLE, BERYL and ALBERT at the counter.

BERYL: *Minnie hasn't touched her milk.*

MYRTLE: *Did you put it down for her?*

BERYL: *Yes, but she never came in for it.*

ALBERT *conversationally: Fond of animals?*

MYRTLE: *In their place.*

ALBERT: *My landlady's got a positive mania for animals — she's
got two cats, one Manx and one ordinary; three rabbits in a hutch
in the kitchen, they belong to her little boy by rights; and one of*

them foolish-looking dogs with hair over his eyes.
MYRTLE: *I don't know to what breed you refer.*
ALBERT: *I don't think it knows itself. . . .*

Cut to LAURA, as she glances at the clock, and collects her parcels in a leisurely manner.

MYRTLE off: *Go and clean off Number Three, Beryl, I can see the crumbs on it from here.*

LAURA walks over to the door leading to Number 2 platform.

ALBERT off: *What about my other cup? I shall have to be moving — the five-forty will be in in a minute.*

MYRTLE off: *Who's on the gate?*

ALBERT off: *Young William.*

Outside, the express roars into Milford Junction Station.

LAURA is standing on the platform with the windows of the refreshment room behind her. The lights from the express flash across her face as it streaks through Number 2 platform. She suddenly puts her hand to her face as a piece of grit gets into her eye. She takes out a handkerchief and rubs her eye for a few moments, then turns and walks back into the refreshment room.

MYRTLE is in the foreground of the shot. LAURA enters through the door, comes over to the counter and stands beside ALBERT, who is drinking his second cup of tea. She rubs her eye. (*Still*)

LAURA: *Please, could you give me a glass of water? I've got something in my eye and I want to bathe it.*

MYRTLE: *Would you like me to have a look?*

LAURA: *Please don't trouble. I think the water will do it.*

MYRTLE handing her a glass of water: *Here.*

MYRTLE and ALBERT watch in silence as LAURA bathes her eye.

ALBERT: *Bit of coal-dust, I expect.*

MYRTLE: *A man I knew lost the sight of one eye through getting a bit of grit in it.*

ALBERT: *Nasty thing — very nasty.*

MYRTLE as LAURA lifts her head: *Better?*

LAURA obviously in pain: *I'm afraid not — oh!*

ALEC comes in.

ALEC: *Can I help?*

LAURA: *Oh, no please — it's only something in my eye.*

MYRTLE: *Try pulling down your eyelid as far as it'll go.*

25

ALBERT: *And then blow your nose.*
ALEC: *Please let me look. I happen to be a doctor.*
LAURA: *It's very kind of you.*
ALEC: *Turn round to the light, please.*
Close shot of LAURA and ALEC.
ALEC: *Now — look up — now look down — I can see it. Keep still. . . .*
He twists up the corner of his handkerchief and rapidly operates with it.
ALEC: *There. . . .*
LAURA blinking: *Oh, dear — what a relief — it was agonizing.*
ALEC: *It looks like a bit of grit.*
LAURA: *It was when the express went through. Thank you very much indeed.*
ALEC: *Not at all.*
There is the sound of a bell on the platform.
ALBERT off: *There we go — I must run.*
LAURA: *How lucky for me that you happened to be here.*
ALEC: *Anybody could have done it.*
LAURA: *Never mind, you did, and I'm most grateful.*
ALEC: *There's my train — good-bye.*
ALEC leaves the buffet and goes out of the door to Number 3 platform.
Outside, he comes out of the refreshment room and hurries along the platform and down the subway.
LAURA also comes out of the refreshment room door on to Number 4 platform. She idly glances across at the opposite platform and sees ALEC.
He emerges from the subway entrance, walks a few steps. His train pulls into the station and he is hidden from view.
Close-up of LAURA. She watches the train as it draws to a standstill.
LAURA'S VOICE: *. . . That's how it all began — just through me getting a little piece of grit in my eye.*
LAURA looks up as she hears her own train approaching.
A shot of Number 3 and 4 platforms. The engine of ALEC's train is in the background. LAURA's train steams into Number 3 platform, hiding it from view.
From outside the window of LAURA's compartment, we see

LAURA sitting down, opening her book and starting to read.
LAURA'S VOICE: *I completely forgot the whole incident — it didn't mean anything to me at all, at least I didn't think it did.*
There is the sound of a guard's whistle and the train starts to move off. Fade out.
As the screen goes black, we hear LAURA's voice.
LAURA'S VOICE: *The next Thursday I went into Milford again as usual. . . .*

Fade in on Milford High Street where LAURA walks along, carrying a shopping basket. She checks the contents of the basket with a shopping list and, having decided on her next port of call, she quickens her step. Dissolve.
We are inside Boots Chemist. LAURA is walking away from the library section and goes over to a counter with soaps, toothbrushes, etc.
LAURA'S VOICE: *I changed my books at Boots — Miss Lewis had at last managed to get the new Kate O'Brien for me — I believe she'd kept it hidden under the counter for two days! On the way out I bought two new toothbrushes for the children — I like the smell of a chemist's better than any other shop — it's such a mixture of nice things — herbs and scent and soap. . . .*
Close shot of MRS LEFTWICH at the end of the counter.
LAURA'S VOICE: *. . . that awful Mrs Leftwich was at the other end of the counter, wearing one of the silliest hats I've ever seen.*
Cut to LAURA placing the toothbrushes in her shopping bag and leaving the counter.
LAURA'S VOICE: *. . . fortunately she didn't look up, so I got out without her buttonholing me. Just as I stepped out on to the pavement. . . .*
Dissolve to LAURA as she comes out of Boots. ALEC comes by walking rather quickly. He is wearing a turned-down hat. He recognizes her, stops, and raises his hat.
ALEC: *Good morning.*
LAURA jumping slightly: *Oh — good morning.*
ALEC: *How's the eye? (Still)*
LAURA: *Perfectly all right. How kind it was of you to take so much trouble.*
ALEC: *It was no trouble at all.*

27

After a slight pause.

ALEC: *It's clearing up, I think.*

LAURA: *Yes — the sky looks much lighter, doesn't it?*

ALEC: *Well, I must be getting along to the hospital.*

LAURA: *And I must be getting along to the grocer's.*

ALEC with a smile: *What exciting lives we lead, don't we? Good-bye.*

Dissolve to the interior of the subway. It is night time. LAURA is walking along, a little out of breath.

LAURA'S VOICE: *That afternoon I had been to the Palladium as usual, but it was a terribly long film, and when I came out I had had to run nearly all the way to the station.*

LAURA starts to go up the steps leading to Number 3 platform. She comes up the subway on to the platform.

LAURA'S VOICE: *As I came up on to the platform the Churley train was just puffing out.*

Cut to the train leaving Number 4 platform.

Close shot of LAURA, watching the Churley train.

LAURA'S VOICE: *I looked up idly as the windows of the carriages went by, wondering if he was there. . . . I remember this crossing my mind but it was quite unimportant — I was really thinking of other things — the present for your birthday was worrying me rather. It was terribly expensive, but I knew you wanted it, and I'd sort of half taken the plunge and left a deposit on it at Spink and Robson's until the next Thursday. The next Thursday. . . .*

Dissolve to the interior of Spink and Robson. Close-up of a travelling clock with a barometer and dates, all in one. It is standing on a glass show case.

LAURA is looking down at it admiringly.

LAURA'S VOICE: *. . . Well — I squared my conscience by thinking how pleased you would be, and bought it — it was wildly extravagant, I know, but having committed the crime, I suddenly felt reckless and gay. . . . .*

Dissolve to Milford High Street. LAURA walks along the street, carrying a small parcel in her hand. It is a sunny day and she is smiling. A barrel organ is playing.

LAURA'S VOICE: *The sun was out and everybody in the street looked more cheerful than usual — and there was a barrel organ at the corner by Harris's, and you know how I love barrel organs — it was playing 'Let the Great Big World Keep Turning', and I gave the man sixpence and went to the Kardomah for lunch.*

Dissolve to inside of a Kardomah Café. LAURA is sitting at an alcove table. A waitress is just finishing taking her order.

LAURA'S VOICE: *It was very full, but two people had got up from the table just as I had come in — that was a bit of luck, wasn't it? Or was it? Just after I had given my order, I saw him come in. He looked a little tired, I thought, and there was nowhere for him to sit, so I smiled and said . . .*

LAURA: *Good morning.*

Close-up of ALEC.

ALEC: *Good morning. Are you alone?*

Resume on LAURA and ALEC.

LAURA: *Yes, I am.*

ALEC: *Would you mind very much if I shared your table — it's very full and there doesn't seem to be anywhere else?*

LAURA moving a couple of parcels and her bag: *Of course not.*

ALEC hangs up his hat and mackintosh and sits down next to her.

ALEC: *I'm afraid we haven't been properly introduced — my name's Alec Harvey.*

LAURA shaking hands: *How do you do — mine's Laura Jesson.*

ALEC: *Mrs or Miss?*

LAURA: *Mrs. You're a doctor, aren't you? I remember you said you were that day in the refreshment room.*

ALEC: *Yes — not a very interesting doctor — just an ordinary G.P. My practice is in Churley.*

A waitress comes to the table.

WAITRESS: *Can I take your order?*

ALEC to LAURA: *What did you plump for?*

LAURA: *The soup and the fried sole.*

ALEC to WAITRESS: *The same for me, please.*

WAITRESS: *Anything to drink?*

ALEC: *No, thank you.*

ALEC pauses and looks at LAURA.

ALEC: *That is — would you like anything to drink?*

LAURA: *No, thank you — just plain water.*

ALEC to WAITRESS: *Plain water, please.*

29

As the WAITRESS goes away, a Ladies Orchestra starts to play very loudly. LAURA jumps.

Cut to a view of the Ladies Orchestra. They are playing with enthusiasm.

Close shot of LAURA and ALEC. They both laugh. ALEC catches LAURA's eye and nods towards the cellist.

Close shot of the cellist. She is a particularly industrious member of the orchestra.

LAURA'S VOICE: *I'd seen that woman playing the cello hundreds of times, but I've never noticed before how funny she looked.*

Close shot of LAURA and ALEC.

LAURA: *It really is dreadful, isn't it — but we shouldn't laugh — they might see us.*

ALEC: *There should be a society for the prevention of cruelty to musical instruments — you don't play the piano, I hope?*

LAURA: *I was forced to as a child.*

ALEC: *You haven't kept it up?*

LAURA smiling: *No — my husband isn't musical at all.*

ALEC: *Bless him!*

LAURA: *For all you know, I might have a tremendous, burning professional talent.*

ALEC shaking his head: *Oh dear, no.*

LAURA: *Why are you so sure?*

ALEC: *You're too sane — and uncomplicated!*

LAURA fishing in her bag for her powder puff: *I suppose it's a good thing to be so uncomplicated — but it does sound a little dull.*

ALEC: *You could never be dull.*

LAURA: *Do you come here every Thursday?*

ALEC: *Yes, to spend a day in the hospital. Stephen Lynn — he's the chief physician here — graduated with me. I take over from him once a week — it gives him a chance to go up to London and me a chance to study the hospital patients.*

LAURA: *I see.*

ALEC: *Do you?*

LAURA: *Do I what?*

ALEC: *Come here every Thursday?*

LAURA: *Yes — I do the week's shopping, change my library book, have a little lunch, and generally go to the pictures. Not a very exciting routine, really, but it makes a change.*

ALEC: *Are you going to the pictures this afternoon?*

LAURA: *Yes.*

ALEC: *How extraordinary — so am I.*

LAURA: *But I thought you had to work all day in the hospital.*

ALEC: *Well, between ourselves, I killed two patients this morning by accident and the Matron's very displeased with me. I simply daren't go back. . . .*

LAURA: *How can you be so silly. . . .*

ALEC: *Seriously — I really did get through most of my work this morning — it won't matter a bit if I play truant. Would you mind very much if I came to the pictures with you?*

LAURA hesitatingly: *Well — I. . . .*

ALEC: *I could sit downstairs and you could sit upstairs.*

LAURA: *Upstairs is too expensive.*

She smiles. The orchestra stops playing.

LAURA'S VOICE: *The orchestra stopped as abruptly as it had started, and we began to laugh again, and I suddenly realized that I was enjoying myself so very much.*

The WAITRESS arrives back with the soup.

LAURA'S VOICE: *I had no premonitions although I suppose I should have had. It all seemed so natural — and so — so innocent.*

Close-up of ALEC over LAURA's shoulder, followed quickly by a close-up of LAURA over ALEC's shoulder.

Dissolve to close shot of the luncheon bill on a plate. ALEC's hand comes into view and picks it up. LAURA's hand tries to take it from him.

LAURA'S VOICE: *We finished lunch, and the idiot of a waitress had put the bill all on one.*

Close shot of LAURA and ALEC.

ALEC: *I really must insist.*

LAURA: *I couldn't possibly.*

ALEC: *Having forced my company on you, it's only fair that I should pay through the nose for it!*

LAURA: *Please don't insist — I would so much rather we halved it, really I would — please.*

ALEC: *I shall give in gracefully.*

LAURA'S VOICE: *We halved it meticulously — we even halved the tip.*

LAURA and ALEC get up from the table and the orchestra plays again. They start laughing as they leave the restaurant.

Dissolve to Milford High Street. The camera tracks with LAURA and ALEC as they are walking along.

LAURA: *We have two choices — ' The Loves of Cardinal Richelieu ' at the Palace, and ' Love in a Mist ' at the Palladium.*

ALEC: *You're very knowledgeable.*

LAURA: *There must be no argument about buying the tickets we each pay for ourselves.*

ALEC: *You must think me a very poor doctor if I can't afford a couple of one and ninepennies!*

LAURA: *I insist.*

ALEC: *I had hoped that you were going to treat me!*

LAURA: *Which is it to be — Palace or Palladium?*

ALEC with decision: *Palladium, I was once very sick on a channel steamer called ' Cardinal Richelieu '.*

Dissolve to inside of the cinema where we see the Palladium Proscenium. On the screen a trailer is being shown, advertising a coming attraction. Superimposed over four spectacular shots in ever increasing sizes, are the following words, which zoom up towards the audience:

STUPENDOUS! COLOSSAL!!
GIGANTIC!!! EPOCH-MAKING!!!!

A burst of flame appears, followed by the title of the picture ' Flame of Passion ' coming shortly. The trailer ends abruptly and the first of a series of advertisements is flashed on the screen. It is a drawing of a pram with the words:

BUY YOUR PRAM AT BURTONS
22, MILFORD HIGH STREET.

Close shot of LAURA and ALEC who are seated in the middle of the front row of the circle. A beam of light from the projector forms the background of the scene.

LAURA leaning forward over the edge of the circle: *I feel awfully grand perched up here — it was very extravagant of you.*

ALEC: *It was a famous victory.*

LAURA: *Do you feel guilty at all? I do.*

ALEC: *Guilty?*

LAURA: *You ought to more than me really — you neglected your work this afternoon.*

ALEC: *I worked this morning — a little relaxation never did any harm to anyone. Why should either of us feel guilty?*

LAURA: *I don't know.*

ALEC: *How awfully nice you are.*

There is a deafening peal of organ music.

With ALEC and LAURA in the foreground, a woman organist rises from the depths of the orchestra pit, organ and all, playing away as though her life depended on it.

Close shot of LAURA and ALEC, as they are watching the organist. A surprised look appears on both their faces. They look at each other, then lean forward to get a better view of the organist.

Close shot of the organist, acknowledging the applause from the audience. She is the woman that plays the cello at the Kardomah Café.

Close shot of LAURA and ALEC.

LAURA: *It can't be.*

ALEC: *It is.*

They both roar with laughter.

Dissolve to Milford Junction Station, showing the yard and booking hall. It is night time. The camera tracks with LAURA and ALEC, who are walking across the station yard.

LAURA'S VOICE: *We walked back to the station. Just as we were approaching the barrier he put his hand under my arm. I didn't notice it then, but I remember it now.* •

LAURA: *What's she like, your wife?*

ALEC: *Madeleine? Oh — small, dark, rather delicate —*

LAURA: *How funny — I should have thought she would be fair.*

ALEC: *And your husband — what's he like?*

They enter the lighted booking hall.

LAURA: *Medium height, brown hair, kindly, unemotional, and not delicate at all.*

ALEC: *You said that proudly.*

LAURA: *Did I?*

They pass the ticket barrier, where ALBERT is on duty, and out on to Number 1 platform.

LAURA: *We've just got time for a cup of tea before our trains go.*

Dissolve to the refreshment room. From behind the counter,

MYRTLE and BERYL are seen gossiping in the foreground, wh
ALEC and LAURA enter through the door. LAURA goes over to
table out of shot. ALEC comes forward to the counter.

MYRTLE: *And for the third time in one week he brought th
common man and his wife to the house without so much as by yo
leave.* To ALEC: *Yes?*

ALEC: *Two teas, please.*

MYRTLE: *Cakes or pastry?*

LAURA off: *No, thank you.*

ALEC: *Are those Bath buns fresh?*

MYRTLE: *Certainly they are — made this morning.*

ALEC: *Two, please.*

MYRTLE puts two Bath buns on a plate. Meanwhile BERYL h
drawn two cups of tea.

MYRTLE: *That'll be sevenpence.*

ALEC: *All right.*

He pays her.

MYRTLE: *Take the tea to the table, Beryl.*

ALEC: *I'll carry the buns.*

LAURA has now seated herself at a table. BERYL brings the te
while ALEC follows with the buns.

ALEC: *You must eat one of these — fresh this morning.*

LAURA: *Very fattening.*

ALEC: *I don't hold with such foolishness.*

BERYL goes out of view towards the counter.

BERYL off: *What happened then, Mrs Bagot?*

LAURA gives ALEC a nudge to draw his attention to MYRTL
and BERYL.

Close shot of MYRTLE and BERYL behind the counter.

MYRTLE slightly relaxed in manner: *Well — it's all very faine,
said, expecting me to do this, that and the other, but what do I ge
out of it? You can't expect me to be a cook-housekeeper and cha
rolled into one during the day, and a loving wife in the evening, jus
because you feel like it. Oh, dear, no. There are just as good fish i
the sea, I said, as ever came out of it, and I packed my boxes the
and there and left him.*

BERYL: *Didn't you never go back?*

MYRTLE: *Never, I went to my sister's place at Folkestone for a bit
and then I went in with a friend of mine and we opened a tea-shop*

34

in Hythe.

BERYL: *And what happened to him?*

MYRTLE: *Dead as a doornail inside three years.*

BERYL: *Well, I never.*

Close shot of LAURA and ALEC.

LAURA: *Is tea bad for one? Worse than coffee, I mean?*

ALEC: *If this is a professional interview my fee is a guinea.*

LAURA: *Why did you become a doctor?*

ALEC: *That's a long story. Perhaps because I'm a bit of an idealist.*

LAURA: *I suppose all doctors ought to have ideals, really — otherwise I should think their work would be unbearable.*

ALEC: *Surely you're not encouraging me to talk shop?*

LAURA: *Why shouldn't you talk shop? It's what interests you most, isn't it?*

ALEC: *Yes — it is. I'm terribly ambitious really — not ambitious for myself so much as for my special pigeon.*

LAURA: *What is your special pigeon?*

ALEC: *Preventative medicine.*

LAURA: *Oh, I see.*

ALEC laughing: *I'm afraid you don't.*

LAURA: *I was trying to be intelligent.*

ALEC: *Most good doctors, especially when they're young, have private dreams — that's the best part of them; sometimes, though, those get over-professionalized and strangulated and — am I boring you?*

LAURA: *No — I don't quite understand — but you're not boring me.*

ALEC: *What I mean is this — all good doctors must be primarily enthusiastic. They must have, like writers and painters and priests, a sense of vocation — a deep-rooted, unsentimental desire to do good.*

LAURA: *Yes — I see that.*

ALEC: *Well, obviously one way of preventing disease is worth fifty ways of curing it — that's where my ideal comes in — preventative medicine isn't anything to do with medicine at all, really — it's concerned with conditions, living conditions and common sense and hygiene. For instance, my speciality is pneumoconiosis.*

LAURA: *Oh, dear!*

ALEC: *Don't be alarmed, it's simpler than it sounds — it's nothing but a slow process of fibrosis of the lung due to the inhalation of particles of dust. In the hospital here there are splendid opportunities for observing cures and making notes, because of the coal-mines.*

LAURA: *You suddenly look much younger.*

ALEC brought up short: *Do I?*

LAURA: *Almost like a little boy.*

ALEC: *What made you say that?*

LAURA staring at him: *I don't know — yes, I do.*

ALEC gently: *Tell me.*

LAURA with panic in her voice: *Oh, no — I couldn't really. You were saying about the coal-mines.*

ALEC looking into her eyes: *Yes — the inhalation of coal-dust — that's one specific form of the disease — it's called anthracosis.*

LAURA hypnotized: *What are the others?*

ALEC: *Chalicosis — that comes from metal-dust — steel-works, you know. . . .*

LAURA: *Yes, of course. Steel-works.*

ALEC: *And silicosis — stone-dust — that's gold-mines.*

LAURA almost in a whisper: *I see.*

There is the sound of a bell.

LAURA: *That's your train.*

ALEC looking down: *Yes.*

LAURA: *You mustn't miss it.*

ALEC: *No.*

LAURA again with panic in her voice: *What's the matter?*

ALEC with an effort: *Nothing — nothing at all.*

LAURA socially: *It's been so very nice — I've enjoyed my afternoon enormously.*

ALEC: *I'm so glad — so have I. I apologize for boring you with those long medical words.*

LAURA: *I feel dull and stupid, not to be able to understand more.*

ALEC: *Shall I see you again?*

There is the sound of a train approaching.

LAURA: *It's the other platform, isn't it? You'll have to run. Don't worry about me — mine's due in a few minutes.*

ALEC: *Shall I see you again?*

LAURA: *Of course — perhaps you could come over to Ketchworth one Sunday. It's rather far, I know, but we should be delighted to see you.*

ALEC intensely: *Please — please. . . .*

The train is heard drawing to a standstill. . . .

LAURA: *What is it?*

ALEC: *Next Thursday — the same time.*

LAURA: *No — I can't possibly — I. . . .*

ALEC: *Please — I ask you most humbly. . . .*

LAURA: *You'll miss your train!*

ALEC: *All right.*

He gets up.

LAURA: *Run. . . .*

ALEC taking her hand: *Good-bye.*

LAURA breathlessly: *I'll be there.*

ALEC: *Thank you, my dear.*

He leaves LAURA, and the camera tracks into a big close shot to hold her, smiling with joy.

LAURA collects her shopping basket and goes towards the door to Number 3 platform.

She comes out of the refreshment room on to the platform. She looks up past camera at ALEC's train, which can be heard pulling out of the station.

A shot of ALEC, from LAURA's view-point. He is leaning out of a carriage window, and waves to her as the train starts to pull out of the station.

Close-up of LAURA. She waves back, and her eyes follow the departing train.

LAURA's VOICE: *I stood there and watched his train draw out of the station. I stared after it until its little red tail light had vanished into the darkness. I imagined him arriving at Churley and giving up his ticket and walking through the streets, and letting himself into his house with his latchkey. Madeleine, his wife, would probably be in the hall to meet him — or perhaps upstairs in her room — not feeling very well — small, dark and rather delicate — I wondered if he'd say ' I met such a nice woman in the Kardomah — we had lunch and went to the pictures ' — then suddenly I knew that he wouldn't — I knew beyond a shadow of doubt that he wouldn't say a word, and at that moment the first awful feeling of danger swept over me.*

A cloud of steam from an incoming engine blows across the screen, almost obscuring LAURA. The grinding of brakes and

37

hiss of steam as her train draws to a standstill, interrupts her thoughts. She walks out of view towards the train.

Through the clearing steam we see her enter a third-class compartment, crowded with people.

She sits down between two other passengers, and glances around the carriage.

LAURA'S VOICE: *I looked hurriedly around the carriage to see if anyone was looking at me.*

The camera pans along the passengers seated on the opposite side of the carriage.

LAURA'S VOICE: *. . . as though they could read my secret thoughts. Nobody was looking at me except a clergyman in the opposite corner.*

The clergyman catches her eye and turns his head away.

Close-up of LAURA as she opens her library book.

LAURA'S VOICE: *I felt myself blushing and opened my library book and pretended to read.*

The train gives a jerk as it starts to move off.

Dissolve to Ketchworth Station, where LAURA walks along the platform towards the barrier. There are several other passengers around her.

LAURA'S VOICE: *By the time we got to Ketchworth, I had made up my mind definitely that I wouldn't see Alec any more.*

A WOMAN'S VOICE: *Good evening, Mrs Jesson.*

LAURA does not hear.

LAURA'S VOICE: *It was silly and undignified flirting like that with a complete stranger.*

She walks on a pace or two, then turns.

LAURA: *Oh — oh — good evening.*

Dissolve to LAURA's house. She walks up the path to the front door.

LAURA'S VOICE: *I walked up to the house quite briskly and cheerfully. I had been behaving like an idiot admittedly, but after all no harm had been done.*

LAURA opens the front door.

She enters the hall, and looks up towards the stairs.

LAURA'S VOICE: *You met me in the hall. Your face was strained and worried and my heart sank.*

LAURA: *Fred, what's the matter?*

Cut to FRED, who walks down the stairs into the hall.

FRED: *It's all right, old girl, but you've got to keep calm and not be upset.*

LAURA: *What is it? What's wrong?*

FRED: *It's Bobbie — he was knocked down by a car on the way home from school. . . .*

LAURA gives a little cry.

FRED: *It's not serious — he was just grazed by the mudguard but it knocked him against the kerb and he's got slight concussion — the doctor's upstairs with him now. . . .*

LAURA flings down her parcels and book and goes upstairs at a run, tearing off her coat as she goes. FRED follows.

Through the open door of the night nursery we see LAURA arrive on the landing and hurry towards the room. She stops in the doorway as she sees the doctor standing beside BOBBIE's bed. BOBBIE is lying with his eyes shut, and his head and right arm bandaged. The doctor puts his fingers to his lips.

DOCTOR: *It's all right, Mrs Jesson — nothing to worry about — he'll be as right as rain in a few hours.*

LAURA goes across the room and kneels at the side of BOBBIE's bed. The DOCTOR now becomes an unimportant part of the scene; his legs only being visible.

LAURA whispering: *You're sure — you're sure it's not serious?*

DOCTOR smiling: *Quite sure — but it was certainly a very lucky escape.*

The DOCTOR moves off out of view.

DOCTOR off: *I've given him a little sedative, and I should advise keeping him at home for a couple of days. It must have been a bit of a shock and his right arm is rather badly bruised.*

The DOCTOR's voice gradually fades away.

LAURA's VOICE: *I felt so dreadful, Fred — looking at him lying there with that bandage round his head. I tried not to show it, but I was quite hysterical inside as though the whole thing were my fault — a sort of punishment — an awful, sinister warning.*

Dissolve to LAURA and BOBBIE. She is seated on his bed, as the maid comes into view and hands BOBBIE a plate of bread and milk.

LAURA's VOICE: *An hour or two later, of course, everything became quite normal again. He began to enjoy the whole thing thoroughly, and revelled in the fact that he was the centre of attraction. Do you remember how we spent the whole evening planning his future?*

Dissolve to FRED and LAURA in the library. They are seated on either side of the fire. FRED is on the sofa with a crossword puzzle and LAURA is smoking a cigarette.

LAURA: *But he's much too young to decide really.*

FRED: *It's a good life — and if the boy has a feeling for it.* . . . .

LAURA: *How can we possibly really know that he has a feeling for it? He'll probably want to be an engine driver next week.*

FRED: *It was last week that he wanted to be an engine driver.*

LAURA: *But it seems so final somehow, entering a child of that age for the Navy.*

FRED: *It's a healthy life.*

LAURA with slight exasperation: *I know it's a good life, dear, and I know that he'll be able to see the world, and have a wife in every port and keep on calling everybody ' sir ' — but what about us?*

FRED: *How do you mean? ' What about us? '*

LAURA: *We shall hardly ever see him.* . . . .

FRED: *Nonsense.*

LAURA: *It isn't nonsense. He'll be sent away to sea as a smooth-faced boy, and the next thing we know he'll be walking in with a long beard and a parrot.*

FRED: *I think you take rather a Victorian view of the Navy, my dear.*

LAURA: *He's our only son and I should like to be there while he's growing up.*

FRED: *All right, old girl. We'll put him into an office and you can see him off on the eight-fifty every morning.*

LAURA crushing her cigarette out: *You really are very annoying — you know perfectly well that I should hate that.*

LAURA rises and goes round to the sofa table, behind FRED. On the table is a work basket, out of which she starts to take some wool, etc.

FRED: *All right — all right, have it your own way.*

After a pause we resume on close-ups of FRED and LAURA, individually.

LAURA suddenly: *Fred.* . . . .

FRED busily counting spaces: *Yes —*

LAURA: *I had lunch with a strange man to-day and he took me to the movies.*

FRED: *Good for you.*

LAURA: *He's awfully nice — he's a doctor. . . .*

FRED rather abstractedly filling in a word: *A — very — noble — profession. . . .*

LAURA helplessly: *Oh dear!*

FRED: *It was Richard the Third who said ' My kingdom for a horse ', wasn't it?*

LAURA: *Yes, dear.*

FRED: *Well, all I can say is that I wish he hadn't — it ruins everything.*

LAURA: *I thought perhaps we might ask him over to dine one evening. . . .*

FRED: *By all means.* He looks up. *Who?*

LAURA: *Doctor Harvey. The one I was telling you about.*

FRED: *Must it be dinner?*

LAURA: *You're never at home for lunch.*

FRED: *Exactly.*

LAURA leaves the table and goes over to sit beside FRED.

LAURA starting to laugh, almost hysterically: *Oh, Fred!*

Close shot of FRED and LAURA.

FRED looking up: *What on earth's the matter?*

LAURA laughing more: *It's nothing — it's only that. . . .*

She breaks off and goes on laughing helplessly until she has to wipe her eyes.

LAURA: *Oh, Fred. . . .*

FRED: *I really don't see what's so terribly funny.*

LAURA: *I do — it's all right, darling, I'm not laughing at you — I'm laughing at me, I'm the one that's funny — I'm an absolute idiot — worrying myself about things that don't really exist — making mountains out of molehills. . . .*

FRED: *I told you when you came in that it wasn't anything serious — there was no need for you to get into such a state. . . .*

LAURA: *No — I see that now — I really do. . . .*

She goes on laughing.

Dissolve to interior of the Kardomah Café. LAURA is sitting at the same table; she is alone. The Ladies Orchestra is playing away as usual.

LAURA'S VOICE: *I went to the Kardomah and managed to get the*

*same table. I waited a bit but he didn't come. . . . The ladies'
orchestra was playing away as usual — I looked at the cellist — she
had seemed to be so funny last week, but to-day didn't seem funny
any more — she looked pathetic, poor thing.*

Dissolve to LAURA, who is walking past the hospital.

LAURA'S VOICE: *After lunch I happened to pass by the hospital —
I remember looking up at the windows and wondering if he were
there, and whether something awful had happened to prevent him
turning up.*

Dissolve to the refreshment room. It is night time. LAURA is
leaving the counter, carrying a cup of tea, which MYRTLE has
just poured out for her. She walks over to a table and sits down.

LAURA'S VOICE: *I got to the station earlier than usual. I hadn't
enjoyed the pictures much — it was one of those noisy musical
things and I'm so sick of them — I had come out before it was over.*

MYRTLE comes over to the stove in the centre of the room.
She bends down to put more coal into it. ALBERT GODBY enters
and perceiving her slightly vulnerable position he tiptoes
towards her.

LAURA is watching ALBERT. After a moment there is a loud
smack, off. LAURA smiles.

MYRTLE springs to an upright position.

MYRTLE: *Albert Godby, how dare you?*

ALBERT: *I couldn't resist it.*

MYRTLE: *I'll trouble you to keep your hands to yourself.*

MYRTLE walks out of view towards the counter.

ALBERT: *You're blushing — you look wonderful when you're angry
— like an avenging angel.*

ALBERT follows her.

At the counter we see individual close-ups of MYRTLE and
ALBERT.

MYRTLE: *I'll give you avenging angel — coming in here taking
liberties. . . .*

ALBERT: *I didn't think after what you said last Monday you'd
object to a friendly little slap.*

MYRTLE: *Never you mind about last Monday — I'm on duty now.
A nice thing if Mr Saunders had happened to be looking through
the window.*

ALBERT: *If Mr Saunders is in the 'abit of looking through windows, it's time he saw something worth looking at.*

MYRTLE: *You ought to be ashamed of yourself!*

ALBERT: *It's just high spirits — don't be mad at me.*

MYRTLE: *High spirits indeed! Here, take your tea and be quiet.*

ALBERT: *It's all your fault, anyway.*

MYRTLE: *I don't know what you're referring to, I'm sure.*

ALBERT: *I was thinking of to-night.*

MYRTLE: *If you don't learn to behave yourself there won't be a to-night — or any other night, either. . . .*

ALBERT: *Give us a kiss.*

MYRTLE: *I'll do no such thing. The lady might see us.*

ALBERT: *Just a quick one — across the counter.*

    He grabs her arm across the counter.

MYRTLE: *Albert, stop it!*

ALBERT: *Come on — there's a love.*

MYRTLE: *Let go of me this minute.*

ALBERT: *Come on, just one. . . .*

    They scuffle for a moment, upsetting a neat pile of cakes on to the floor.

MYRTLE: *Now look at me Banburys — all over the floor.*

    ALBERT bends down to pick them up.

    Cut to STANLEY as he enters the door.

STANLEY: *Just in time or born in the vestry.*

    LAURA glances up at the clock, takes up her shopping basket, and during the following dialogue, the camera pans with her to the door which leads to Number 3 platform.

MYRTLE off: *You shut your mouth and help Mr Godby pick up them cakes. Come along, what are you standing there gaping at?*

    LAURA comes out of the refreshment room door on to Number 3 platform.

LAURA'S VOICE: *As I left the refreshment room I saw a train coming in — his train. He wasn't on the platform, and I suddenly felt panic-stricken at the thought of not seeing him again.*

    Dissolve to the subway entrance to Number 2 and 3 platforms.

    ALEC dashes up the steps on to the platform, and runs towards LAURA.

ALEC breathlessly: *Oh, my dear, I'm so sorry — so terribly sorry.*

LAURA: *Quick — your train — you'll miss it.*

    They both rush along the platform towards the subway.

ALEC as they go: *I'd no way of letting you know — the house surgeon had to operate suddenly — it wasn't anything really serious, but I had to stand by as it was one of my special patients.*

Inside the subway LAURA and ALEC are running down the steps.

ALEC: *. . . You do understand, don't you?*

LAURA now rather breathless: *Of course — it doesn't matter a bit.*

They turn the corner at the foot of the steps, and the camera tracks with them as they run along the subway towards Number 4 platform.

ALEC: *I thought of sending a note to the Kardomah, but I thought they would probably never find you, or keep on shouting your name out and embarrass you, and I. . . .*

They start running up the steps leading to Number 4 platform.

LAURA: *Please don't say any more — I really do understand. . . .*

A whistle blows as LAURA and ALEC hurry on to the platform.

LAURA: *Quickly — oh, quickly. The whistle's gone.*

They hurry to the waiting train. ALEC opens the door of a third-class compartment and turns to LAURA.

ALEC: *I'm so relieved that I had a chance to explain — I didn't think I would ever see you again.*

LAURA: *How absurd of you.*

The train starts to move off.

LAURA: *Quickly — quickly. . . .*

ALEC jumps into the train, and leans out of the window. LAURA walks along a few paces with the train.

ALEC: *Next Thursday.*

LAURA: *Yes. Next Thursday.*

The train gradually gains on LAURA, and ALEC goes out of view. LAURA watches ALEC's departing train, waves after it and stands quite still until the sound of it has died away in the distance. A strident voice from the loudspeaker breaks in:

LOUDSPEAKER: *The train for Ketchworth is standing at Number 3 platform.*

LAURA suddenly realizes that she is about to miss her own train, and she makes a dash for the subway steps.

Dissolve to a close shot of LAURA and ALEC sitting in the front row of the circle at the Palladium Cinema. They are both laughing and are obviously very happy. The lights go up.

ALEC: *The stars can change in their courses, the universe go up in flames and the world crash around us, but there'll always be Donald Duck.*

LAURA: *I do love him so, his dreadful energy, his blind frustrated rages. . . .*

The lights begin to dim.

ALEC: *It's the big picture now — here we go — no more laughter — prepare for tears.*

Dissolve to the main title of the big picture, flashed on to the screen. It is the film advertised in the trailer of two weeks ago, ' Flame of Passion '.

LAURA'S VOICE: *It was a terribly bad picture.*

Dissolve to LAURA and ALEC walking up the last few steps of the circle towards the exit. The back of an usherette forms the foreground of the shot.

LAURA'S VOICE: *We crept out before the end, rather furtively, as though we were committing a crime. The usherette at the door looked at us with stony contempt.*

Dissolve to a medium shot of LAURA and ALEC coming out of the cinema. ALEC takes LAURA's arm, as they walk along the street.

LAURA'S VOICE: *It really was a lovely afternoon, and it was a relief to be in the fresh air. Do you know, I believe we should all behave quite differently if we lived in a warm, sunny climate all the time. We shouldn't be so withdrawn and shy and difficult.*

Dissolve to a picturesque shot of ALEC and LAURA as they walk along by the side of a lake.

LAURA'S VOICE: *Oh, Fred, it really was a lovely afternoon. There were some little boys sailing their boats — one of them looked awfully like Bobbie — that should have given me a pang of conscience I know, but it didn't! . . .*

After a few moments ALEC stops walking and turns to LAURA.

LAURA'S VOICE: *Alec suddenly said that he was sick of staring at the water and that he wanted to be on it.*

The foreground of the scene is now composed of one or two rowing boats, which have been covered up for the winter. On the landing stage in the background, a boatman is pushing ALEC and LAURA away from the shore.

LAURA'S VOICE: *All the boats were covered up but we managed to persuade the old man to let us have one.*

Close shot of the boatman.

LAURA'S VOICE: *He thought we were raving mad. Perhaps he was right.*

The boat is in the water, with the boatman in the foreground.

LAURA'S VOICE: *. . . Alec rowed off at a great rate, and I trailed my hand in the water — it was very cold but a lovely feeling.*

ALEC and LAURA are in the boat. LAURA is in the foreground of the shot. ALEC catches a crab and an oar slips out of its rowlock.

LAURA: *You don't row very well, do you?*

ALEC putting the oar back in the rowlock: *I'm going to be perfectly honest with you. I don't row at all, and unless you want to go round in ever narrowing circles, you had better start steering.* (Still)

LAURA laughs and picks up the steering ropes. They start off again.

The boat is following a somewhat erratic course.

LAURA'S VOICE: *We had such fun, Fred. I felt gay and happy and sort of released — that's what's so shameful about it all — that's what would hurt you so much if you knew — that I could feel as intensely as that — away from you — with a stranger.*

The camera is tracking with the boat. LAURA is in the fore-ground of the shot. They are approaching a very low bridge.

LAURA: *Oh, look out . . . we shan't get through.*

ALEC glancing behind: *Pull on your left.*

As the bridge looms nearer and nearer, ALEC rises to his feet. LAURA pulls the wrong rope and looks up inquiringly at ALEC. There is a crash and a shudder as the boat hits the bridge.

LAURA'S VOICE: *I never could tell left from right.*

The boat rocks violently and there is a loud splash. LAURA looks towards the water and begins to laugh.

ALEC is standing in the lake. The water only comes up to his knees. He is very wet.

Close-up of LAURA, who is roaring with laughter.

Dissolve to the interior of the boathouse. ALEC's trousers are hanging over a line in front of an open ' Ideal ' boiler. ALEC himself is seated on an upturned dinghy. He is wearing an overcoat, which is obviously not his own, and is smoking a cigarette. He looks at LAURA.

She is kneeling by the boiler, laying out ALEC's shoes and socks to dry.

She gets up and goes over to a carpenter's bench, where a kettle is boiling on a gas ring. Beside the ring is a bottle of milk and two cups. In the background of the shot are a collection of punts, boats, oars, etc. LAURA starts to make tea.

LAURA: *The British have always been nice to mad people. That boat-man thinks we are quite dotty, but just look how sweet he has been: overcoat, tea, milk — even sugar.*

Close shot of ALEC as he watches her prepare the tea. After a moment we hear the sound of LAURA walking across the boat-house towards ALEC. He follows her with his eyes. Her hand comes into view and gives him a cup of tea.

ALEC: *Thank you.*

LAURA sits down on an old wooden chair, and they both begin to stir their tea.

ALEC quietly: *You know what's happened, don't you?*

LAURA: *Yes — yes, I do.*

ALEC: *I've fallen in love with you.*

LAURA: *Yes — I know.*

ALEC: *Tell me honestly — my dear — please tell me honestly if what I believe is true. . . .*

LAURA in a whisper: *What do you believe?* (Still)

ALEC: *That it's the same with you — that you've fallen in love too.*

LAURA near tears: *It sounds so silly.*

ALEC: *Why?*

LAURA: *I know you so little.*

ALEC: *It is true, though — isn't it?*

LAURA with a sigh: *Yes — it's true.*

ALEC making a slight movement towards her: *Laura. . . .*

LAURA: *No please . . . we must be sensible — please help me to be sensible — we mustn't behave like this — we must forget that we've said what we've said.*

ALEC: *Not yet — not quite yet.*

LAURA panic in her voice: *But we must — don't you see!*

ALEC leaning forward and taking her hand: *Listen — it's too late now to be as sensible as all that — it's too late to forget what we've said — and anyway, whether we'd said it or not couldn't have mattered — we know — we've both of us known for a long time.*

LAURA: *How can you say that — I've only known you for four weeks — we only talked for the first time last Thursday week.*

ALEC: *Last Thursday week. Hadn't it been a long time since then — for you? Answer me truly.*

LAURA: *Yes.*

ALEC: *How often did you decide that you were never going to see me again?*

LAURA: *Several times a day.*

ALEC: *So did I.*

LAURA: *Oh, Alec.*

ALEC: *I love you — I love your wide eyes and the way you smile and your shyness, and the way you laugh at my jokes.*

LAURA: *Please don't. . . .*

ALEC: *I love you — I love you — you love me too — it's no use pretending that it hasn't happened because it has.*

LAURA with tremendous effort: *Yes it has. I don't want to pretend anything either to you or to anyone else . . . but from now on I shall have to. That's what's wrong — don't you see? That's what spoils everything. That's why we must stop here and now talking like this. We are neither of us free to love each other, there is too much in the way. There's still time, if we control ourselves and behave like sensible human beings, there's still time to — to. . . .*

She puts her head down and bursts into tears.

ALEC: *There's no time at all.*

ALEC goes over to her, takes her in his arms and kisses her. Cut to close-up of the station bell, ringing loudly at Milford Junction Station. It is night time.

LAURA and ALEC come on to Number 1 platform from the booking hall.

LAURA: *There's your train.*

ALEC: *Yes.*

LAURA: *I'll come with you — over to the other platform.*

They walk along the platform and down the subway steps.

In the subway ALEC stops and takes her in his arms. She struggles a little.

LAURA: *No dear — please . . . not here — someone will see.*

ALEC kissing her: *I love you so.*

They are interrupted by the sound of feet coming down the subway steps. A shadow appears on the wall behind them. They hurry off through the subway.

In the foreground of the shot, the dim outline of LAURA can be seen. She is watching herself and ALEC as they walk along the subway towards Number 4 platform. The sound of an express train roaring overhead, becomes the sound of loud music. FRED's voice is heard.

FRED's VOICE: *Don't you think we might have that down a bit, darling?*

After a slight pause.

FRED's VOICE: *Hoi — Laura!*

Dissolve to a shot over LAURA's shoulder. The subway has suddenly disappeared, and FRED and the library have taken its place.

LAURA jumping: *Yes, dear?*

FRED: *You were miles away.*

LAURA: *Was I? Yes, I suppose I was.*

FRED rising: *Do you mind if I turn it down a little — it really is deafening. . . .*

He goes towards the radio.

LAURA with an effort: *Of course not.*

She bends down and starts sewing. FRED turns down the radio, and returns to his place.

FRED: *I shan't be long over this, and then we'll go up to bed. You look a bit tired, you know. . . .*

LAURA: *Don't hurry — I'm perfectly happy.*

She continues her sewing for a moment or two, then she looks up again. FRED's head is down, concentrating on the paper.

LAURA passes her hand across her forehead wearily.

LAURA's VOICE: *How can I possibly say that? ' Don't hurry, I'm perfectly happy.' If only it were true. Not, I suppose, that anybody is perfectly happy really, but just to be ordinarily contented — to be at peace. It's such a little while ago really, but it seems an eternity since that train went out of the station — taking him away into the darkness.*

Dissolve to LAURA walking in the subway. The sound of her train is heard pulling in overhead.

LAURA's VOICE: *I went over to the other platform and got into my train as usual.*

Close shot of LAURA in the railway compartment. She is seated in a corner.

LAURA'S VOICE: *This time I didn't attempt to read — even to pretend to read — I didn't care whether people were looking at me or not. I had to think. I should have been utterly wretched and ashamed — I know I should but I wasn't — I felt suddenly quite wildly happy — like a romantic schoolgirl, like a romantic fool! You see he had said he loved me, and I had said I loved him, and it was true — it was true! I imagined him holding me in his arms — I imagined being with him in all sorts of glamorous circumstances. It was one of those absurd fantasies — just like one has when one is a girl — being wooed and married by the ideal of one's dreams — generally a rich and handsome Duke.*

As LAURA turns to look out of the window, the camera tracks and pans slowly forward until the darkened countryside fills the screen.

LAURA'S VOICE: *I stared out of the railway carriage window into the dark and watched the dim trees and the telegraph posts slipping by, and through them I saw Alec and me.*

The countryside fades away and ALEC and LAURA are seen, dancing a gay waltz. The noise of the train recedes, and is replaced by music.

LAURA'S VOICE: *Alec and me — perhaps a little younger than we are now, but just as much in love, and with nothing in the way.*

The sound of the train returns for a moment and the dancing figures fade away. The train noise dies away again, and is replaced by the sound of an orchestra tuning up, as the passing countryside changes to a picture of ALEC and LAURA in a theatre box. ALEC gently takes a beautiful evening cloak from her shoulders and hands her a programme and opera glasses.

LAURA'S VOICE: *I saw us in Paris, in a box at the Opera. The orchestra was tuning up. Then we were in Venice — drifting along the Grand Canal in a gondola.*

LAURA and ALEC are reclining in a gondola. There is the sound of lovely tenor voices and mandolins coming over the water. The scene changes to one of ALEC and LAURA in a car. They are driving through beautiful countryside, and the wind blowing LAURA's hair accentuates the feeling of speed.

50

LAURA'S VOICE: *I saw us travelling far away together; all the places I have always longed to go.*

We now see the rushing wake of a ship; then a ship's rail.

LAURA'S VOICE: *I saw us leaning on the rail of a ship looking at the sea and the stars — standing on some tropical beach in the moonlight with the palm trees sighing above us. Then the palm trees changed into those pollarded willows by the canal just before the level crossing. . . .*

The camera pulls back from the window of the railway compartment and pans to include LAURA.

LAURA'S VOICE: *. . . and all the silly dreams disappeared, and I got out at Ketchworth and gave up my ticket. . . .*

Dissolve to the booking hall and station yard of Ketchworth Station. LAURA gives up her ticket and walks away across the station yard.

LAURA'S VOICE: *. . . and walked home as usual — quite soberly and without any wings at all.*

Dissolve to the interior of LAURA's bedroom. It is night time. LAURA is seated at her dressing table. The camera shoots on to the mirror of the dressing table.

LAURA'S VOICE: *When I had changed for dinner and was doing my face a bit — do you remember? I don't suppose you do, but I do — you see you don't know that that was the first time in our life together that I had ever lied to you — it started then, the shame of the whole thing, the guiltiness, the fear. . . .*

The reflection of FRED can be seen coming into the bedroom. He comes forward and kisses LAURA lightly.

FRED: *Good evening, Mrs Jesson.*

LAURA: *Hullo, dear.*

FRED: *Had a good day?*

LAURA: *Yes, lovely.*

FRED: *What did you do?*

LAURA: *Well — I shopped — and had lunch — and went to the pictures.*

FRED moving away: *All by yourself?*

LAURA in sudden panic: *Yes — no — that is, not exactly.*

FRED cheerfully: *How do you mean, not exactly?*

LAURA with a rush: *Well I went to the pictures by myself, but I*

*had lunch with Mary Norton at the Kardomah — she couldn't come
to the pictures because she had to go and see her in-laws — you
know, they live just outside Milford — so I walked with her to the
bus and then went off on my own.*

FRED: *I haven't seen Mary Norton for ages. How was she looking?*

LAURA: *She was looking very well really — a little fatter, I think. . . .*

FRED: *Hurry up with all this beautifying — I want my dinner.*

LAURA gaily: *Go on down — I shan't be five minutes. . . .*

> FRED goes out. LAURA sits staring at herself in the glass. She
> puts her hand to her throat as if she were suffocating.

> Dissolve to a close shot of LAURA at the telephone.

LAURA on the telephone: *Is Mrs Norton there, please? Yes, I'll hold
on. Hallo, is that you Mary — no — I know — I haven't seen you
for ages. Listen, my dear, will you be a saint and back me up in the
most appalling domestic lie?* She laughs forcedly. *Yes— my life
depends on it. Yesterday I went into Milford as usual to do my
shopping with the special intention of buying a far too expensive
present for Fred's birthday.*

> MARY NORTON is at the other end of the telephone, as she
> stands in the hallway of her house. She is plump and rather
> blousy.

LAURA off: *Well, Spink and Robson's hadn't got what I wanted
which was one of those travelling clocks with the barometer, and
everything in one, but they rang up their branch in Broadham, and
said that there was one there — so I hopped on to the one-thirty
train and went to get it.*

> Resume on LAURA, back in her bedroom.

LAURA: *Now then, this is where the black lie comes in — Fred asked
me last night if I had had a good day in Milford, and I said yes, and
you and I had lunched together at the Kardomah, and that you had
gone off to see your in-laws, and I had gone to the pictures, so if by
any chance you should run into him — don't let me down. All
right?* She laughs again. *Yes, dear, I promise I'll do the same for
you. Yes, that would be lovely. No I can't on Thursday, that's my
Milford day. What about Friday? Very well — perfect — Good-bye.*

> She hangs up the telephone and the social smile on her face
> fades.

> Dissolve to FRED and LAURA's bedroom. The lights are out and
> she is awake, while FRED is asleep.

LAURA'S VOICE: *That week was misery. I went through it in a sort of trance — how odd of you not to have noticed that you were living with a stranger in the house.*

Dissolve to the exterior of the hospital. It is day time. LAURA is walking up and down outside. (*Still*)

LAURA'S VOICE: *Thursday came at last — I had arranged to meet Alec outside the hospital at twelve-thirty.*

ALEC comes out of the main doors of the hospital and down the steps in the background. He sees LAURA and comes up to her.

ALEC almost breathlessly: *Hullo. . . .*

LAURA with a strained smile: *Hullo. . . .*

ALEC: *I thought you wouldn't come — I've been thinking all the week that you wouldn't come.*

LAURA: *I didn't mean to really — but here I am. . . .*

He takes her arm, they turn and walk away together along the road. The camera follows them, shooting on to their backs from a low angle. The background of the scene is composed of rooftops and trees.

Dissolve to the Royal Hotel restaurant where LAURA and ALEC are seated at a corner table. A wine waiter is standing beside ALEC, who is examining the wine list. LAURA is looking around the room.

LAURA'S VOICE: *Do you know, I hadn't been inside the Royal since Violet's wedding reception? It all seemed very grand.*

The wine waiter leaves the table.

LAURA'S VOICE: *He actually ordered a bottle of champagne! And when I protested he said that we were only middle-aged once! We were very gay during lunch and talked about quite ordinary things.*

Close shot of ALEC over LAURA's shoulder.

LAURA'S VOICE: *Oh, Fred, he really was charming — I know you would have liked him if only things had been different.*

Dissolve to the hotel entrance lounge. ALEC and LAURA come into view through the door leading from the restaurant.

LAURA'S VOICE: *As we were going out he said that he had a surprise for me, and that if I would wait in the lounge for five minutes he'd show me what it was.*

ALEC runs down some steps towards the main entrance.

LAURA'S VOICE: *He went out and down the steps at a run — more like an excited schoolboy than a respectable doctor.*

LAURA watches ALEC as he leaves the hotel. She turns and the camera focuses on the restaurant doorway out of which are emerging MARY NORTON and MRS ROLANDSON. MARY NORTON's clothes are reasonably good but carelessly worn. MRS ROLANDSON is over smartly dressed; her hat is too young for her, and she gives the impression of being meticulously enamelled. They both recognize LAURA.

LAURA smiles with agonized amiability.

MARY: *Laura, it was you after all! Hermione said it was you but you know how shortsighted I am — I peered and peered and couldn't be sure.*

LAURA, with a bright fixed expression, shakes hands with them both.

LAURA: *I never saw you at all — how dreadful of me — I expect it was the champagne — I'm not used to champagne at lunch — or for dinner either for the matter of that — but Alec insisted. . . .*

MARY: *Alec who, dear?*

LAURA with a gay little laugh: *Alec Harvey of course. Surely you remember the Harveys — I've known them for years.*

MARY: *I don't think I ever. . . .*

LAURA: *He'll be back in a minute — you'll probably recognize him when you peer at him closely. . . .*

MRS ROLANDSON: *He certainly looked very charming and very attentive!*

LAURA: *He's a dear — one of the nicest people in the world and a wonderful doctor.*

ALEC comes bounding back up the steps, and joins the group.

LAURA flashes him one anguished look and then introduces him.

LAURA: *Alec — you remember Mrs Norton, don't you?*

ALEC politely shaking hands: *I . . . er . . . I'm afraid I. . . .*

MARY: *It's no use Laura — we've never met before in our lives — I'm sure we haven't. . . .*

LAURA: *How absurd — I made certain that he and Madeleine were there when you dined with us just before Christmas — Alec — this is Mrs Rolandson.*

MRS ROLANDSON: *How do you do.*

They shake hands. There is a pause.

54

MRS ROLANDSON: *What horrid weather, isn't it?*

ALEC: *Yes.*

MRS ROLANDSON: *Still, I suppose we can't expect spring at this time of the year, can we?*

ALEC: *No.*

There is another pause.

MARY: *Well, we really must be going — I'm taking Hermione with me to see the in-laws — to give moral support — Good-bye, Doctor Harvey.*

ALEC: *Good-bye.*

They shake hands. (*Still*)

MRS ROLANDSON bowing: *Good-bye. Good-bye, Mrs Jesson.*

LAURA: *Good-bye.*

She smiles pleasantly.

MARY to LAURA: *Good-bye, my dear. I do so envy you and your champagne.*

MARY NORTON and MRS ROLANDSON go out of view towards the steps.

LAURA putting her hands over her face: *That was awful — awful. . . .*

ALEC: *Never mind.*

LAURA: *They had been watching us all through lunch — oh dear. . . .*

ALEC with an attempt at brightness: *Forget it — come out and look at the surprise.*

Dissolve to the exterior of the Royal Hotel. In the foreground of the scene is a small two-seater car, which is parked outside the hotel entrance. ALEC and LAURA come out of the hotel and get into the car.

LAURA'S VOICE: *There at the foot of the steps was a little two-seater car. Alec had borrowed it from Stephen Lynn for the afternoon. We got in in silence and drove away.*

Dissolve to the car driving through the outskirts of Milford.

It pulls up near a small bridge over a stream.

LAURA'S VOICE: *When we were out in the real country — I think it was a few miles beyond Brayfield — we stopped the car just outside a village and got out. There was a little bridge and a stream and the sun was making an effort to come out but really not succeeding very well. We leaned on the parapet of the bridge and looked down into the water. I shivered and Alec put his arm around me.*

LAURA and ALEC are leaning on the bridge, looking down into

the water.

ALEC: *Cold?*

LAURA: *No — not really.*

ALEC: *Happy?*

LAURA: *No — not really.*

ALEC: *I know what you're going to say — that it isn't worth it — that the furtiveness and the necessary lying outweigh the happiness we might have together — wasn't that it?*

LAURA: *Yes. Something like that.*

ALEC: *I want to ask you something — just to reassure myself.*

LAURA her eyes filling with tears: *What is it?*

ALEC: *It is true for you, isn't it? This overwhelming feeling that we have for each other — it is as true for you as it is for me — isn't it?*

LAURA: *Yes — it's true.*

She bursts into tears and ALEC puts his arms closer around her. They stand in silence for a moment and then kiss each other passionately.

Dissolve to another shot of LAURA and ALEC. They are now again leaning on the bridge.

LAURA'S VOICE: *I don't remember how long we stayed on that bridge or what we said. I only remember feeling that I was on the edge of a precipice, terrified yet wanting desperately to throw myself over.*

ALEC and LAURA start to move towards the car.

LAURA'S VOICE: *Finally we got back into the car and arrived at Stephen Lynn's garage just as it was getting dark.*

Dissolve to the inside of a small lock-up garage. The camera is shooting towards the entrance. The car drives into the garage towards the camera and stops. The headlights are turned off and ALEC and LAURA get out. They are silhouetted against the entrance, behind which are the lighted windows of the block of flats.

LAURA'S VOICE: *We put the car away and Alec said he had to leave the keys of the car in Stephen Lynn's flat, and suggested that I came up with him. I refused rather too vehemently. Alec reminded me that Stephen wasn't coming back till late, but I still refused.*

ALEC shuts the garage doors.

Dissolve to the exterior of station approach. LAURA and ALEC are walking along towards the camera. In the background of the scene is a signal box and railway lines. An express can be heard approaching in the distance.

ALEC stopping: *I'm going to miss my train. I'm going back.*

LAURA: *Back where?*

ALEC: *To Stephen's flat.*

LAURA: *Oh, Alec.*

They look at each other as the noise of the express rises to a thundering crescendo out of which emerges the scream of the train whistle.

The express hurtles into the tunnel.

LAURA and ALEC are in each other's arms.

LAURA pushing him away in panic: *I must go now. I really must go home.*

She runs off out of view. ALEC stands watching her.

We see LAURA entering the booking hall, from ALEC's viewpoint.

ALEC turns and walks away.

In the refreshment room LAURA takes a cup of tea over to her usual table.

LAURA'S VOICE: *I got my cup of tea at the counter, and went over to our usual table. Two soldiers came in and started to make a scene at the counter.*

LAURA sits at the table, sipping her tea. Her face looks strained and exhausted.

Cut to MYRTLE, BERYL and the two soldiers, BILL and JOHNNIE, who have just arrived at the counter.

BILL: *Afternoon, lady.*

MYRTLE grandly: *Good afternoon.*

BILL: *A couple of splashes, please.*

MYRTLE: *Very sorry, it's out of hours.*

BILL: *Just sneak us a couple under cover of them poor old sandwiches.*

MYRTLE: *Them sandwiches were fresh this morning, and I shall do no such thing.*

BILL: *Come on, be a sport. You could pop it into a couple of teacups.*

MYRTLE: *You can have as much as you want after six o'clock.*

JOHNNIE: *My throat's like a parrot's cage — listen!*

He makes a crackling noise with his throat.

MYRTLE: *I'm sorry — my licence does not permit me to serve alcohol out of hours — that's final! You wouldn't want me to get into trouble, would you?*

BILL: *Give us a chance, lady, that's all — just give us a chance.*

They both roar with laughter.

MYRTLE: *Beryl, ask Mr Godby to come 'ere for a moment, will you?*

BERYL: *Yes, Mrs Bagot.*

She runs out of view towards the platform.

BILL: *Who's 'e when 'e's at home?*

MYRTLE: *You'll soon see — coming in here cheeking me.*

JOHNNIE: *Come off it, mother, be a pal!*

MYRTLE losing her temper: *I'll give you mother, you saucy upstart*

BILL: *Who are you calling an upstart!*

MYRTLE: *You — and I'll trouble you to get out of here double quick — disturbing the customers and making a nuisance of your selves.*

JOHNNIE: *'Ere, where's the fire — where's the fire?*

ALBERT enters the refreshment room with BERYL.

ALBERT: *What's going on in 'ere?*

He walks towards the counter.

MYRTLE with dignity: *Mr Godby, these gentlemen are annoying me.*

BILL: *We haven't done anything.*

JOHNNIE: *All we did was ask for a couple of drinks. . . .*

MYRTLE: *They insulted me, Mr Godby.*

JOHNNIE: *We never did nothing of the sort — just 'aving a little joke, that's all.*

ALBERT laconically: *'Op it — both of you.*

BILL: *We've got a right to stay 'ere as long as we like.*

ALBERT: *You 'eard what I said — 'op it!*

JOHNNIE: *What is this, a free country or a bloomin' Sunday school?*

ALBERT firmly: *I checked your passes at the gate — your train's due in a minute — Number 2 platform — 'op it.*

JOHNNIE: *Look 'ere now. . . .*

BILL: *Come on, Johnnie — don't argue with the poor basket.*

ALBERT dangerously: *'Op it!*

BILL and JOHNNIE walk towards the door. JOHNNIE turns.

JOHNNIE: *Toodle-oo, mother, and if them sandwiches were made this morning, you're Shirley Temple. . . .*

They go out.

Resume on ALBERT, MYRTLE and BERYL.

MYRTLE: *Thank you, Albert.*

BERYL: *What a nerve, talking to you like that!*

MYRTLE: *Be quiet, Beryl — pour me out a nip of Three Star — I'm feeling quite upset.*

ALBERT: *I've got to get back to the gate.*

MYRTLE graciously: *I'll be seeing you later, Albert.*

ALBERT with a wink: *Okay!*

ALBERT goes out of view. BERYL brings MYRTLE a glass of brandy.

Close shot of LAURA. A train bell goes. She fumbles in her bag and finds a cigarette. She lights it. There is the sound of her train approaching.

LOUDSPEAKER ANNOUNCEMENT: *The train now arriving at platform five is the five forty-three for Ketchworth.*

Train noise is heard.

LAURA's VOICE: *I really must go home.*

ALEC's VOICE: *I'm going back to the flat.*

LAURA's VOICE: *I must go home now, I really must go home.*

ALEC's VOICE: *I'm going back to the flat.*

LAURA's VOICE: *I'm going home.*

MYRTLE off: *There's the five forty-three.*

LAURA sits, puffing her cigarette, listening to her train draw into the station. Suddenly she rises, crushes out her cigarette, grabs her bag, and runs to the door leading to Number 3 platform. She runs across the platform and gets into her train.

Entering a third-class compartment, she sits down next to two women.

She is in a nervous state of indecision. The Guard's whistle blows. After a second or two she suddenly jumps up, and stumbles over the women sitting next to her.

LAURA muttering: *Excuse me, I have forgotten something.*

She gets out of the train, just as it begins to move off. The camera pans with her as she runs along the platform with the train gathering speed behind her. She runs out of shot towards the barrier, leaving a view of the train as it steams away from the station.

Dissolve to the main entrance hallway and staircase of a block of flats. LAURA comes in from the street. It is raining. She pauses for a moment to examine a board on which are listed the names of the tenants and their flat numbers. She walks up the stairs to the door of Stephen Lynn's flat on the second floor, and rings the bell. ALEC opens the door, and she goes quickly past him into the hall almost without looking at him.

ALEC softly: *Oh, darling, I didn't dare to hope.*

ALEC leads her gently through to the sitting room. It is rather a bleak little room. The furniture looks impersonal. He has lit the fire, but it hasn't had time to get under way and is smoking. They stand quite still for a moment, looking at each other.

LAURA: *It's raining.*

ALEC his eyes never moving from her face: *Is it?*

LAURA: *It started just as I turned out of the High Street.*

ALEC: *You had no umbrella and your coat's wet. . . .*

He gently helps her off with her coat.

ALEC: *You mustn't catch cold — that would never do.*

LAURA looking at herself in the glass over the mantelpiece, and slowly taking off her hat: *I look an absolute fright.*

ALEC taking her hat and her scarf: *Let me put these down.*

LAURA: *Thank you.*

ALEC putting them on a chair near the writing desk with the coat: *I hope the fire will perk up in a few minutes. . . .*

LAURA: *I expect the wood was damp.*

ALEC ruefully: *Yes — I expect it was.*

There is silence.

ALEC: *Do sit down, darling. . . .*

LAURA sits down on the sofa.

LAURA with an attempt at gaiety: *I got right into the train and then got out again — wasn't that idiotic?*

ALEC sitting down next to her and taking her in his arms: *We're both very foolish.*

He kisses her.

LAURA weakly: *Alec — I can't stay you know — really, I can't.*

ALEC: *Just a little while — just a little while. . . .*

There is the sound of the lift gates clanging. They both break apart and look up.

From their view-point we see the flat hallway. There is the sound of a step outside on the landing, and then the sound of a key fitted into the front door.

LAURA and ALEC jump to their feet.

LAURA in a frantic whisper: *Quickly — quickly — I must go.* . . .

ALEC snatches up her hat and coat and pushes them into her hand.

ALEC: *Here — through the kitchen — there's a tradesmen's staircase.* . . .

They rush into the small kitchen where there is a door opening on to the fire escape. ALEC tears it open. LAURA runs through it on to a metal staircase, without even looking back. She disappears down the stairs. ALEC shuts the door quietly after her and leans against it for a moment with his eyes closed.

A MAN's VOICE from the sitting room: *Is that you, Alec?*

ALEC as casually as he can: *Yes.*

He starts to walk back into the sitting room.

STEPHEN LYNN is standing by the entrance to the hall. He is a thin, rather ascetic-looking man. ALEC walks towards him.

ALEC: *You are back early.*

STEPHEN: *I felt a cold coming on so I denied myself the always questionable pleasure of dining with that arch arguer Roger Hinchley, and decided to come back to bed.* Walking to the chair by the writing desk: *Inflamed membranes are unsympathetic to dialectic —*

ALEC: *What will you do about food?*

STEPHEN smiling: *I can ring down to the restaurant later on if I want anything — we live in a modern age and this is a service flat.*

ALEC with a forced laugh: *Yes — Yes — I know.*

STEPHEN still smiling: *It caters for all tastes.*

He lightly flicks LAURA's scarf off the chair and hands it to ALEC.

STEPHEN: *You know, Alec, my dear, you have hidden depths that I never even suspected.*

ALEC: *Look here, Stephen, I really.* . . .

STEPHEN holding up his hand: *For heaven's sake, Alec, no explanations or apologies — I am the one who should apologize for having returned so inopportunely — it is quite obvious to me that you were interviewing a patient privately — women are frequently neurotic creatures, and the hospital atmosphere upsets them. From the rather undignified scuffling I heard when I came into the hall, I gather that she beat a hurried retreat down the backstairs. I'm surprised at this*

61

farcical streak in your nature, Alec — such carryings on were quite unnecessary — after all, we have known each other for years and I am the most broad-minded of men.

ALEC *stiffly: I'm really very sorry, Stephen. I'm sure that the whole situation must seem inexpressibly vulgar to you. Actually it isn't in the least. However, you are perfectly right — explanations are unnecessary — particularly between old friends. I must go now.*

STEPHEN *still smiling: Very well.*

ALEC: *I'll collect my hat and coat in the hall. Good-bye.*

STEPHEN: *Perhaps you'd let me have my latch key back? I only have two and I'm so afraid of losing them — you know how absent-minded I am.*

ALEC *giving him the key: You're very angry, aren't you? (Still)*

STEPHEN: *No, Alec — not angry — just disappointed.*

ALEC goes out without another word.

In the street outside, the camera is tracking on a close shot of LAURA's legs and feet. She is running fast along the pavement. It is pouring with rain.

Close-up of LAURA, who is still running. The background of the scene is composed of the tops of houses. As she approaches a lamp post, the light increases on her face and dies away quickly as she passes it.

The camera tracks to the pavement from LAURA's angle. Her shadow becomes large and elongated as she moves further away from the lamp post.

Resume on LAURA as she approaches another lamp post. She is out of breath and slows down to a walk.

LAURA'S VOICE: *I ran until I couldn't run any longer — I leant against a lamp post to try to get my breath — I was in one of those side-roads that lead out of the High Street. I know it was stupid to run, but I couldn't help myself.*

Close shot of LAURA as she leans against the lamp post.

LAURA'S VOICE: *I felt so utterly humiliated and defeated and so dreadfully, dreadfully ashamed. After a moment or two I pulled myself together, and walked on in the direction of the station.*

The camera starts to track with her along the street.

LAURA'S VOICE: *It was still raining but not very much. I suddenly realized that I couldn't go home, not until I had got myself under*

*more control, and had a little time to think. Then I thought of you
waiting at home for me, and the dinner being spoilt.*

LAURA is now at the telephone in a tobacconist's shop. She
looks pale and bedraggled.

LAURA'S VOICE: *So I went into the High Street and found a tobacconist and telephoned to you — do you remember — ?*

LAURA at the telephone (*Still*): *Fred — is that you?* With a tremendous effort she makes her voice sound ordinary: *Yes, dear — it's
me — Laura — Yes — of course everything's perfectly all right, but I
shan't be home to dinner — I'm with Miss Lewis, dear — the
librarian at Boots I told you about — I can't explain in any detail
now because she's just outside the telephone box — but I met her
a little while ago in the High Street in the most awful state — her
mother has just been taken ill, and I've promised to stay with her
until the doctor comes — Yes, dear, I know, but she's always been
tremendously kind to me and I'm desperately sorry for her — No —
I'll get a sandwich — tell Ethel to leave a little soup for me in a
saucepan in the kitchen — Yes, of course — as soon as I can. Good-
bye.*

She hangs up the telephone.

LAURA'S VOICE: *It's awfully easy to lie — when you know that you're
trusted implicitly — so very easy, and so very degrading.*

She walks slowly out of the telephone box.

The camera is shooting from a high angle on to a road leading
off the High Street. It has stopped raining but the pavement is
still wet and glistening. LAURA is slowly walking towards the
camera.

LAURA'S VOICE: *I started walking without much purpose — I turned
out of the High Street almost immediately — I was terrified that I
might run into Alec — I was pretty certain that he'd come after me
to the station.*

The camera is shooting down on to another street. LAURA is
still walking.

LAURA'S VOICE: *I walked for a long while. . . .*

Dissolve to a shot of the war memorial. The foreground of the
shot is composed of part of the war memorial statue: a soldier's
hand gripping a bayoneted service rifle. Beyond it LAURA is seen
as a tiny figure walking towards a seat near the base of the
memorial.

63

LAURA'S VOICE: *Finally, I found myself at the war memorial — you know it's right at the other side of the town. It had stopped raining altogether, and I felt stiflingly hot so I sat down on one of the seats.*

Close shot of LAURA on the seat.

LAURA'S VOICE: *There was nobody about, and I lit a cigarette (Still) — I know how you disapprove of women smoking in the street — I do too, really — but I wanted to calm my nerves and I thought it might help.*

She is now in profile to the camera, and has finished her cigarette.

LAURA'S VOICE: *I sat there for ages — I don't know how long — then I noticed a policeman walking up and down a little way off — he was looking at me rather suspiciously. Presently he came up to me.*

The POLICEMAN walks up into a shot over LAURA's shoulder.

POLICEMAN: *Feeling all right, Miss?*

LAURA faintly: *Yes, thank you.*

POLICEMAN: *Waiting for someone?*

LAURA: *No — I'm not waiting for anyone.*

POLICEMAN: *You don't want to go and catch cold you know — that would never do. It's a damp night to be sitting about on seats, you know.*

LAURA rising: *I'm going now anyhow — I have a train to catch.*

Close shot of LAURA and the POLICEMAN.

POLICEMAN: *You're sure you feel quite all right?*

LAURA: *Yes — quite sure — good night.*

POLICEMAN: *Good night, Miss.*

As LAURA walks off the camera pans and tracks with her, shooting at her back.

LAURA'S VOICE: *I walked away — trying to look casual — knowing that he was watching me. I felt like a criminal. I walked rather quickly back in the direction of the High Street.*

Dissolve to Milford Junction Station. The clock on platforms 2 and 3 forms the foreground of shot. The time is six minutes to ten. LAURA comes up out of the subway in the background and walks along the platform. The station is not very well lit, and there is hardly anyone about.

LAURA'S VOICE: *I got to the station fifteen minutes before the last*

*train to Ketchworth, and then I realized that I had been wandering
about for over three hours, but it didn't seem to be any time at all.*

LAURA comes into the refreshment room.

It is nearly closing time, and the room is half-lighted. There is
the melancholy noise of a goods train chugging through the
station. BERYL is draping the things on the counter with muslin
cloths while STANLEY, wearing his ordinary clothes, stands
gossiping with her. LAURA comes in through the door in the
background.

BERYL: *Stan, you are awful!*

STANLEY: *I'll wait for you in the yard.*

BERYL: *Oh, all right.*

STANLEY goes out.

LAURA: *I'd like a glass of brandy, please.*

BERYL: *We're just closing.*

LAURA: *I see you are, but you're not quite closed yet, are you?*

BERYL sullenly: *Three Star?*

LAURA: *Yes, that'll do.*

BERYL getting it: *Tenpence, please.*

LAURA taking money from her bag: *Here — and — have you a piece
of paper and an envelope?*

BERYL: *I'm afraid you'll have to get that at the bookstall.*

LAURA: *The bookstall's shut — please — it's very important — I
should be so much obliged.* . . .

BERYL: *Oh, all right — wait a minute.*

BERYL goes out.

LAURA sips the brandy at the counter. She is obviously trying
to control her nerves. After a moment BERYL can be heard
walking back across the refreshment room. She enters the shot
and puts down some notepaper and an envelope.

LAURA: *Thank you so much.*

BERYL: *We close in a few minutes, you know.*

LAURA: *Yes, I know.*

BERYL goes out of shot and the camera pans with LAURA as she
takes a few paces along the counter in order to be under the
light. She stares at the paper for a moment, takes another sip
of brandy, and then begins to write.

BERYL looks at LAURA with exasperation.

Close shot of LAURA. BERYL can be heard walking away across

the refreshment room and slamming the door at the other end. LAURA falters in her writing, then breaks down and buries her face in her hands. In the background the door to the platform opens and ALEC comes in. He looks hopelessly round for a moment, then, seeing her, walks forward.

ALEC: *Thank God — Oh, darling. . . .*

LAURA: *Please go away — please don't say anything. . . .*

ALEC: *I've been looking for you everywhere — I've watched every train.*

LAURA: *Please go away. . . .*

ALEC: *You're being dreadfully cruel. It was just a beastly accident that he came back early — he doesn't know who you are — he never even saw you.*

LAURA: *I suppose he laughed, didn't he?* Bitterly. *I suppose you spoke of me together as men of the world?*

ALEC: *We didn't speak of you — we spoke of a nameless creature who had no reality at all.*

LAURA: *Why didn't you tell him who I was? Why didn't you tell him we were cheap and low and without courage — why didn't you. . . .*

ALEC: *Stop it, Laura — pull yourself together.*

LAURA: *It's true! Don't you see? It's true. . . .*

ALEC: *We know we really love each other — that's true — that's all that really matters.*

LAURA: *It isn't all that matters — other things matter too, self-respect matters, and decency — I can't go on any longer.*

ALEC: *Could you really say good-bye — not see me any more?*

LAURA: *Yes — if you'd help me.*

ALEC after a pause: *I love you, Laura — I shall love you always until the end of my life — all the shame that the world might force on us couldn't touch the real truth of it. I can't look at you now because I know something — I know that this is the beginning of the end — not the end of my loving you — but the end of our being together. But not quite yet, darling — please not quite yet.*

LAURA in a dead voice: *Very well — not quite yet.*

ALEC: *I know what you feel about this evening — I mean about the beastliness of it. I know about the strain of our different lives; our lives apart from each other. The feeling of guilt, of doing wrong is a little too strong, isn't it? Too persistent? Perhaps too great a price to pay for the few hours of happiness we get out of it. I know all this because it's the same for me too.*

LAURA: *You can look at me now — I'm all right.*

ALEC looking at her: *Let's be careful — let's prepare ourselves — a sudden break now, however brave and admirable, would be too cruel. We can't do such violence to our hearts and minds.*

LAURA: *Very well.*

ALEC: *I'm going away.*

LAURA: *I see.*

ALEC: *But not quite yet.*

LAURA: *Please — not quite yet.*

A train bell goes.

The door leading to the staff-room opens and BERYL comes in.

BERYL: *That's the ten-ten. It's after closing time.*

ALEC: *Oh, it is?*

BERYL: *I shall have to lock up.*

BERYL escorts LAURA and ALEC to the door of Number 3 platform. They go out and the camera remains on BERYL as she slams the door and bolts up.

Outside, LAURA and ALEC walk up and down the platform.

ALEC: *I want you to promise me something.*

LAURA: *What is it?*

ALEC: *Promise me that however unhappy you are, and however much you think things over, that you'll meet me next Thursday.*

LAURA: *Where?*

ALEC: *Outside the hospital — twelve-thirty?*

LAURA: *All right — I promise.*

ALEC: *I've got to talk to you — I've got to explain.*

LAURA: *About going away?*

ALEC: *Yes.*

LAURA: *Where are you going? Where can you go? You can't give up your practice.*

ALEC: *I've had a job offered me. I wasn't going to tell you — I wasn't going to take it — but I know now, that it's the only way out.*

LAURA: *Where?*

ALEC: *A long way away — Johannesburg.*

LAURA stopping still: *Oh, Alec. . . .*

ALEC: *My brother's out there. They're opening a new hospital —*

they want me in it — it's a fine opportunity really. I'll take Madeleine and the boys. It's been torturing me — the necessity of making a decision one way or the other. I haven't told anybody — not even Madeleine. I couldn't bear the idea of leaving you — but now I see, it's got to happen soon anyway — it's almost happening already.

LAURA: *When will you go?*

ALEC: *Almost immediately — in about two weeks' time.*

LAURA: *It's quite near, isn't it?*

ALEC: *Do you want me to stay? Do you want me to turn down the offer?*

LAURA: *Don't be foolish, Alec.*

ALEC: *I'll do whatever you say.*

LAURA her eyes filling with tears: *That's unkind of you, my darling.*
    Close-up of the station loudspeaker.

LOUDSPEAKER: *The train for Ketchworth, Longdean and Perford is now entering Number Three platform.*
    A train can be heard entering the station.
    Dissolve to LAURA and ALEC. He opens the door of an empty third-class compartment and LAURA gets in. ALEC shuts the door after her and LAURA leans out of the open window. (*Still*)

ALEC: *You're not angry with me, are you?*

LAURA: *No, I'm not angry — I don't think I'm anything really — I feel just tired.*

ALEC: *Forgive me.*

LAURA: *Forgive you for what?*
    Close-up of ALEC over LAURA's shoulder.

ALEC: *For everything — for having met you in the first place — for taking the piece of grit out of your eye — for loving you — for bringing you so much misery.*
    Close-up of LAURA over ALEC's shoulder.

LAURA trying to smile: *I'll forgive you — if you'll forgive me.*
    Close-up of ALEC over LAURA's shoulder. There is the sound of the guard's whistle and the train starts to move. The camera and LAURA track away from ALEC as he stands staring after the train which pulls out of the station. Fade out.

LAURA'S VOICE: *All that was a week ago — it is hardly credible that it should be so short a time.*

Fade in on hospital. It is day time. LAURA is standing by a lamp

68

post in the foreground of the shot. After a moment ALEC comes down the hospital steps and joins her.

LAURA'S VOICE: *To-day was our last day together. Our very last together in all our lives. I met him outside the hospital as I had promised at 12.30 — this morning — at 12.30 this morning — that was only this morning.*

Dissolve to ALEC and LAURA sitting in a car.

LAURA'S VOICE: *We drove into the country again, but this time he hired a car. I lit cigarettes for him every now and then as we went along. We didn't talk much — I felt numbed and hardly alive at all. We had lunch in the village pub.*

Dissolve to ALEC and LAURA leaning over the bridge. The car is parked nearby.

LAURA'S VOICE: *Afterwards we went to the same bridge over the stream — the bridge that we had been to before.*

Cut to Milford Junction Station and yard. It is night time. LAURA and ALEC are crossing the station yard towards the booking hall. (*Still*)

LAURA'S VOICE: *Those last few hours together went by so quickly. We walked across the station yard in silence and went into the refreshment room.*

ALEC and LAURA are sitting at the refreshment room table. The voices of ALBERT and MYRTLE fade away to a murmur in the background.

ALEC: *Are you all right, darling?*

LAURA: *Yes, I'm all right.*

ALEC: *I wish I could think of something to say.*

LAURA: *It doesn't matter — not saying anything, I mean.*

ALEC: *I'll miss my train and wait to see you into yours.*

LAURA: *No — no — please don't. I'll come over to your platform with you — I'd rather.*

ALEC: *Very well.*

LAURA: *Do you think we shall ever see each other again?*

ALEC: *I don't know.* His voice breaks. *Not for years anyway.*

LAURA: *The children will all be grown up — I wonder if they'll ever meet and know each other.*

ALEC: *Couldn't I write to you — just once in a while?*

LAURA: *No — please not — we promised we wouldn't.*

ALEC: *Laura, dear, I do love you so very much. I love you with all my heart and soul.*

LAURA *without emotion: I want to die — if only I could die.*

ALEC: *If you died you'd forget me — I want to be remembered.*

LAURA: *Yes, I know — I do too.*

ALEC *glancing at the clock: We've still got a few minutes.*

DOLLY *off: Laura! What a lovely surprise!*

LAURA *dazed: Oh, Dolly!*

> DOLLY *joins* LAURA *and* ALEC.

DOLLY: *My dear, I've been shopping till I'm dropping. My feet are nearly falling off, and my throat's parched, I thought of having tea in Spindle's, but I was terrified of losing the train.*

LAURA'S VOICE: *It was cruel of Fate to be against us right up to the last minute. Dolly Messiter — poor, well-meaning, irritating Dolly Messiter. . . .*

> The camera is slowly tracking in to a close-up of LAURA.

DOLLY: *I'm always missing trains and being late for meals, and Bob gets disagreeable for days at a time.* Her voice is fading away. *He's been getting those dreadful headaches, you know. I've tried to make him see a doctor but he won't.*

> Her voice fades out.

LAURA'S VOICE: *. . . crashing into those last few precious minutes we had together. She chattered and fussed, but I didn't hear what she said. I was dazed and bewildered. Alec behaved so beautifully — with such perfect politeness. Nobody could have guessed what he was really feeling — then the bell went for his train.*

> The platform bell rings.

LAURA: *There's your train.*

ALEC: *Yes, I know.*

DOLLY: *Aren't you coming with us?*

ALEC: *No, I go in the opposite direction. My practice is in Churley.*

DOLLY: *Oh, I see.*

ALEC: *I am a general practitioner at the moment.*

LAURA *dully: Doctor Harvey is going out to Africa next week.*

DOLLY: *Oh, how thrilling.*

> There is the sound of ALEC's train approaching.

ALEC: *I must go.*

LAURA: *Yes, you must.*

ALEC: *Good-bye.*

DOLLY: *Good-bye.*

He shakes hands with DOLLY, and looks swiftly once only at LAURA.

Close-up of LAURA. ALEC's hand comes into the shot and gives her shoulder a little squeeze.

LAURA'S VOICE: *I felt the touch of his hand for a moment and then he walked away. . . .*

ALEC is seen from LAURA's view-point. He crosses the refreshment room and goes out of the door on to the platform.

LAURA'S VOICE: *. . . away — out of my life for ever.*

Close shot of LAURA and DOLLY. LAURA is gazing out of the door through which ALEC has just passed. She seems almost unaware of DOLLY at her side, who proceeds to fumble in her handbag for lipstick and a mirror. DOLLY is chattering, but we do not hear her voice.

LAURA'S VOICE: *Dolly still went on talking, but I wasn't listening to her — I was listening for the sound of his train starting — then it did. . . .*

The sound of ALEC's train is heard as it starts to move out of the station.

Close-up of LAURA.

LAURA'S VOICE: *I said to myself — 'He didn't go — at the last minute his courage failed him — he couldn't have gone — at any moment now he'll come into the refreshment room again pretending that he'd forgotten something.' I prayed for him to do that — just so I could see him once more — for an instant — but the minutes went by. . . .*

There is the sound of the station bell.

Close shot of LAURA and DOLLY.

DOLLY: *Is that the train?*

She addresses MYRTLE.

DOLLY: *Can you tell me, is that the Ketchworth train?*

MYRTLE off: *No, that's the express.*

LAURA: *The boat-train.*

DOLLY: *Oh, yes — that doesn't stop, does it?*

DOLLY gets up and moves out of shot towards the counter.

LAURA jumps to her feet and rushes blindly out of the door leading to Number 2 platform. As the camera pans to the door it goes off level, giving the effect of LAURA running uphill. She runs out of the refreshment room towards the camera and the railway lines.

The railway lines are seen from above. An express train hurtles through the scene. The camera is tilted.

Close-up of LAURA from a low angle. She is swaying on the edge of the platform. The lights from the express streak past her face. The noise is deafening. She stands quite still. The lights stop flashing across her face and the sound of the train dies away rapidly. Slowly the camera returns to a normal angle.

LAURA'S VOICE: *I meant to do it, Fred, I really meant to do it — I stood there trembling — right on the edge — but then, just in time I stepped back — I couldn't — I wasn't brave enough — I should like to be able to say that it was the thought of you and the children that prevented me — but it wasn't — I had no thoughts at all — only an overwhelming desire not to be unhappy any more — not to feel anything ever again. I turned and went back into the refreshment room — that's when I nearly fainted. . . .*

Dissolve to the library at LAURA's house. It is night time. Close-up of LAURA, who is sitting with her sewing in her lap. She is staring straight in front of her.

Close-up of FRED, who is looking at her. He continues to look at her in silence for a moment or two.

FRED gently: *Laura!*

She doesn't answer. He gets up.

Close shot of LAURA. FRED kneels beside her and softly touches her hand.

FRED: *Laura. . . .*

LAURA turning her head slowly and looking at him — her voice sounds dead: *Yes, dear?*

FRED: *Whatever your dream was — it wasn't a very happy one, was it?*

LAURA in a whisper: *No.*

FRED: *Is there anything I can do to help?*

LAURA: *Yes, my dear — you always help. . . .*

FRED: *You've been a long way away?*

LAURA nodding, her eyes fill with tears: *Yes, Fred.*

FRED moves a little closer to her and quietly rests his face against her hand.

FRED with a catch in his voice: *Thank you for coming back to me.*
Fade out.